The Second Journey

ALSO BY JOAN ANDERSON

A Year by the Sea

An Unfinished Marriage

A Walk on the Beach

A Weekend to Change Your Life

VOICE

Hyperion · New York

To Andrew and Luke . . .

*Gratitude for the lessons you
offered me during the first journey
in preparation for the second*

CONTENTS

Ten Years Later

...one small thing
I've learned these years,

how to be alone,
and at the edge of aloneness
how to be found by the world.

Innocence is what we allow
to be gifted back to us
once we've given ourselves away.

There is one world only,
the one to which we gave ourselves
utterly, and to which one day

we are blessed to return.

David Whyte
from
The House of Belonging

PROLOGUE

Most of us, halfway to a hundred, confront a need for greater self-awareness. We reach a point when the power of youth is gone, the possibility of failure presents itself, and the dreams of earlier times seem shallow and pointless. And then we find ourselves asking the tough questions: What am I meant to do now? What really matters? Who am I?

For many years I had ignored these questions because I had too many responsibilities—too many other lives to consider. But all of a sudden, there were no more excuses. Old truths and ideals no longer served me. I was restless, unhappy, and full of an undefined ache, standing at a crossroads with no clear idea of what path to follow. I only knew that I needed a change. So I took a leap of faith, walked away from the mainstream of life, and dove headlong into the unknown.

My first book, *A Year by the Sea*, tells about the "awakening" I experienced when I left behind my husband and family to live on Cape Cod. It is a very personal memoir that has helped hundreds of thousands of women wake up as well. But the itinerary I designed for myself during that year alone proved difficult to hold on to once I returned to living with others. It was one thing to live a simple life, guided by the cycles of nature and my own inner tides while I walked the beaches of Cape Cod and cooked dinner for one, quite another to do so once I resumed my place in the web of family and friends, and a career.

This book chronicles the ten years from that time of "awakening" to the more recent past, when I finally began to feel settled into my own reality. In the process of eliminating illusion, I was able once and for all to embrace what is simple and true. By looking back at the roads I chose to travel, I came to see how many were valid and how many were not—those that I happened upon quite by accident where lessons were learned and hardships endured, and those that led to counterfeit destinations that in the short term seemed attractive but in the long term proved catastrophic.

It is my hope that through my sharing of pitfalls and triumphs, you will be encouraged to create your own new itinerary, knowing all the while that detours, back roads, and slippery causeways are all parts of the journey as well as its lessons. But how do such journeys begin?

The call to a second journey usually commences when unexpected change is thrust upon you, causing a crisis of feelings so great that you are stopped in your tracks. Personal events such as a betrayal, a diagnosis of serious illness, the death of a loved one, loss of self-esteem, a fall from power are only a few of the catalysts. A woman caught thusly has no choice but to pause, isolate, even relocate until she can reevaluate the direction in which she should head. Should she stay the course or choose another path?

But alas, many of us inhibit our capacity for growth

because the culture encourages us to live lives of uniformity. We stall, deny, ignore the ensuing crisis because of confusion, malaise, and yes, even propriety. Yet more and more, I come in contact with women, particularly in midlife—that uneasy and ill-defined period—who do not want merely to be stagnant but rather desire to be generative. Today's woman has the urge to go against the prevailing currents, step out of line, and break with a polite society that has her following the unwritten rules of relationship, accepting the abuses of power in the workplace, and blithely living with myriad *shoulds* when she has her own burgeoning desires.

This book will help you navigate through change—from being merely awakened to being a determined, impassioned pilgrim on her own individual path. This does not mean giving up family and friends; it simply means integrating the web of family and other relationships into your world so that they are a part of your life but not your entire life.

During my travels or life experiences, I was made to account for that which was outlived in my life and that which was unlived. By gradually letting go of that which was finished or outlived, I was able to make room for and welcome new endeavors and yet-unlived possibilities.

We are born to be ourselves—in need of upgrading the gene—to look back again and again and befriend that person we once intended to become. Life, like a beach, is always rearranging itself. The trick is to welcome and then work with, not against, the changes, and in doing so deepen our innate strengths. Knowing, acknowledging, and celebrating the phases all women go through—how we've risen above our angst, respecting our very determination—that is the fodder needed to continue our independent journeys. The goal is to come of age in the middle of life rather than live out our days lacking purpose and energy. It's all about rearranging our lives in our own image.

The Second Journey

1

Dead End

September

*The actual arrival at a goal always creates a turmoil
unconnected to any previous imaginings.*

—David Whyte

It is a glittering September morning, and I am sitting on a deck at the edge of a salt marsh, coffee cup in hand, feet up on the railing, relaxed and more than ready for a morning of catch-up with Ro and Susan, two of my closest friends on Cape Cod. I take a deep breath, gaze out at the marsh grass, now turning burnt orange as the sun climbs higher, and remember why I love the Cape so much—especially this particular spot, where if the wind is blowing just right, I can hear the roar of the Atlantic in the distance. Here, in a moment such as this, I feel an abiding sense of harmony. Everything is right with the world.

"So," Susan begins as soon as the basket of croissants has been around once, "you've finally made it to the porch—first time in three months." I turn sharply away from the landscape and toward the note of sarcasm I hear in her voice, and I am startled to see severe looks on both her and Ro's faces.

"What are you talking about?" I ask, and then I take a gulp of coffee and wait for an answer that is not forthcoming. I was in the mood for a long overdue social gathering, one of those leisurely mornings we used to share regularly before the chain of appearances associated with promoting my last book and writing the new one got in the way. But it is obvious that they are preparing to take me to task. I know the signs all too well. Lately it seems I can't keep anyone happy. At the end of August, after the annual family gathering, my kids left complaining that I had seemed distracted the whole time they were here; my ninety-one-year-old mother stops by every morning and sighs loudly when I remind her I have to work; and my agent is forever pestering me about impending deadlines. No matter how hard or how fast I pedal, I constantly feel as if I am slipping backward as I head uphill.

"You two know how much work I have right now," I say with more than a hint of frustration. Both used to hold high-pressure jobs before retiring to Cape Cod. Susan had been a television producer and Ro a marketing executive. Both women had also raised children and sustained marriages. They came to the Cape tired, worn out, and ready for adventure. We've kayaked, hiked the Cape's beaches, shopped, and shared a lifetime's worth of secrets. They are usually sympathetic to my schedule, and they are the first people I call when I am stuck and need a good trek through the woods to sort out my thoughts. So I am surprised at the sharpness in the air.

"This is about more than your work, Joan," Ro says. "If I lived in the three-ring circus you do, I wouldn't be able to produce a thing. That's what's got us worried—you seem to be your own worst enemy right now. You've become a glutton—always putting more on your plate than you can possibly handle—and the overload is killing you. For God's sakes, look at you. When was the last time you got your hair streaked—probably before your last book tour. You certainly don't take that kind of time just for yourself anymore."

"You've written three books and delivered countless inspirational talks urging women to rid themselves of the deference to other people's expectations, yet here you are, dancing furiously to a tune of others," Susan adds. "It's kind of weird—don't you think?"

She's right. I've been fitting in my personal life and needs around my work ever since *A Year by the Sea* became a best-seller—on top of which I've had five grandchildren arrive, a husband retire, and my mother go through a series of eye and stomach surgeries. There is never enough of me to go around. So while I would prefer to laugh their comments away, I can't. Instead I bite my tongue and turn back toward the marsh, where a mother osprey is coaxing her babies to fly, and feel the peace I seek whenever I am in the presence of something wild and natural.

"Don't go passive on us," Ro says, picking up on my subtle withdrawal.

"I'm not. I'm just concentrating on what you're saying. It's kind of profound for early morning." The high spirits I brought to the porch are beginning to plummet. I've been up and down a lot lately, relaxed and expansive, like I felt a minute ago, and falling precipitously into exhaustion and gloom. I know that this moodiness is just one more by-product of a cluttered calendar, but I am truly at a loss for what to change. When I wrote my first book, I had no idea success would be so busy. At one point, I naïvely thought it would mean more freedom, but I've learned that I am only as good as my latest sales figures. The trouble is, I like what I do. Sure I spend more time talking on the phone, returning e-mails, meeting with fans and business associates, and whatever else it takes to promote my work than I do actually writing, but I'm glad to feel so productive and fulfilled.

"Look, I'm doing the best I can," I answer defensively. Besides, it's easy for them to point their fingers; they are both retired, with comfortable financial packages and lots of free time on their hands. My husband retired on the early side, and his educator's pension doesn't always reach far enough.

"We just want you to get your priorities straight," Susan continues, sounding a tad patronizing. "Remember, we've been there. Both of us let our work suck the life out of us, and we just want to help you before it's too late. Whatever I was chasing at my job was always a hair out of reach."

"My job was just the same," Ro chimes in. "Before I retired, my life was like a Dilbert cartoon with irritable bowel syndrome. I never had a chance to recharge. We would no sooner finish one marketing campaign than the next would begin. Everything was about the deadline— never my personal deadlines, mind you, but the deadlines set by the marketplace. I tried for a while to justify all the imbalance with illusions about the good service my company provided for people. But those excuses all disappeared when the personal products company I worked for bought Ben and Jerry's ice cream and Slim-Fast on the same day. My first reaction was, I gave my forties and fifties for that? Joan, neither of us wants you to repeat our mistakes."

"So, it is time to ask yourself just what is driving you: the money or the message?" Susan pushes on. "You toss around amazing nuggets of wisdom, but are you living your message? Ro is right—you look haggard and tired."

"Well, thanks for the compliment," I say, dumbfounded by her frankness and at a loss as to how to reply. Like most good friends, they have been in on too many of my secrets, but I'm not ready to declare defeat. There are so many differences between their corporate work experiences and the life I am living, and there is still so much I want to do. I just have to become more organized and gain a little more control over my schedule. I reach for another croissant.

I am curious, though, about why they are suddenly so riled up. I remember hearing a sitcom star say at the close of her long-running show that she hoped to get back all of the friendships she hadn't had time for when she was working. Is that what is going on right now?

"Do you guys feel as though I've left you out somehow?" I ask.

"No," Ro says too quickly for my liking. "We feel that you are cutting yourself out of your life—giving it away and taking none of the goodies for yourself. It's got to be damn lonely being you—best-seller aside. You are chained to your computer, and when you do go away, it's to an empty hotel room."

"Yes, we do miss you," Susan adds. "We don't care about your competency, or your Amazon numbers—what happened to plain old Joan—the loosey-goosey woman who parties hard, skinny-dips in the moonlight, and drinks too much wine?"

I remember that woman, too, and the memory makes me smile. Still, this morning's mood has turned, and now I feel awkward. I want to remain aloof and pretend, somehow, that they are talking about someone else, not me. Ro must sense my discomfort, because she quickly switches from pointing out the problem to proposing a solution.

"So here's the deal. I'm making you sign back up for the gym," she insists, passing me the registration card she just happens to have tucked in her back pocket.

"And I'm going to drag you to tai chi," Susan adds.

I look at both of them aghast. I am willing to admit that I need to slow down and make some time for myself. But I have to clean up my desk and plan this new book, not add exercise lessons to the docket. It is true that life, as I am living it, has lost its luster. But today, all I wanted was a beautiful sunrise, the quiet company of good friends, and a chance to catch my breath.

I make my way to the door, give them each a hug, and thank them for their suggestions. On the drive home I'm overwhelmed by unpleasant thoughts, not the least of which is a recurrent dream I have been having recently. In the dream, I am standing in the basement of our home—which, because of its age, has a dirt foundation. I am convinced I've murdered someone—and buried her in the corner. I visit the grave each day, praying that the body will decompose quickly so that my crime will go undiscovered. But there is never any change. When I wake up, I am always anxious, and I feel certain that I've committed the crime. Could it be that the person I have killed is myself?

Truth, like anything else, can be picked up or left alone depending upon your frame of mind. Right now I am willing to hear what my friends are saying, but I don't have the strength for prolonged self-scrutiny. Besides, there must be some small adjustments I can make that won't require a complete rethinking of my life. Any more radical overhauls will have to wait until I've finished this manuscript and gotten through the next few months of booked retreats. Still, deep down I know that the measure of my continuing identity must come from refusing to be swallowed by my goals. Having chosen my own set of complications, I have no one to blame but myself.

The light turns red and I come to a stop. I promise myself I'll analyze my calendar and begin to eliminate anything that seems superfluous—lunches that are purely social, meetings where I have no leadership responsibilities, parties that aren't appealing. I'll clear my desk of would-be writers' unsolicited manuscripts, refrain from answering the phone until the afternoon, and attempt to get help for my mother. The simple act of coming up with a few immediate, manageable solutions gives me comfort. When the light turns green, I push the gas pedal a little harder than is necessary. Everything will be fine.

TWO WEEKS LATER I finally make it to my internist, only because she won't renew a prescription unless I make an appointment. I've never enjoyed going to the doctor, and sitting here half naked in a cold, sterile examining room, waiting has me half crazed. Doctors seem to be in the business of trying to find things wrong with their patients, and since everyone has been pointing a finger at my lifestyle, I am more than certain the doctor, too, will find something to pick on. I hear the doorknob turn and brace myself.

I chose Dr. Pressman because she is a woman, recommends yoga rather than tranquilizers, is intelligent yet sensitive, and most of all, because she seems mortal. One of the things I like most about her is that she always seems to have enough time to talk a bit; her gentle, genuine questions and the fact that she remembers details about my life I forgot I even shared always settle me down. This time is no different, and as we babble for a few minutes, I start to relax. But then she slides back on track and gets to the real business at hand . . . my blood pressure. It had been elevated some months back and she had put me on a mild diuretic, told me to do more aerobic exercise, cut back on the wine, and lose ten pounds. Aside from the exercise, I didn't much heed her instructions.

"My God, Joan, what have you been up to?" she says, as the blood pressure cup releases its air. "Your pressure is higher than last time."

I try to sound nonchalant, although I can see her eyes register alarm.

"Nothing out of the ordinary," I say, attempting to sound casual.

"Oh?" she mumbles, while scribbling her findings onto my chart. "Didn't you just come back from a book tour? Where did you go this time?"

"All over the place. I ended up in Philadelphia. Other than that it's hard to distinguish one place from another."

"Really?" she says, peering over the rim of her glasses with a critical glare. "Did you ever think that might be a sign that perhaps you have too much on your plate?"

"Don't we all," I joke.

"No, I'm serious, Joan. These numbers are scary. You are going to need to rethink your priorities." There's that word again. This conversation is beginning to sound all too familiar.

"Well, I'd be hard-pressed to cut anything out," I snap back. "I'm off to speak in Connecticut today, and I have a pretty full calendar throughout the fall. I can't just up and quit."

"Well, you'd better figure it out. Your entire cardiovascular system is at stake. This issue isn't reversible, but it is controllable. I'm ordering a stress test to be done next week, and you'll need to see our nutritionist—your sugar levels look suspicious, too. Here are some prescriptions," she continues, ripping the papers off her pad. "I want you to have an EKG. Take everything off down to your waist and put on this johnny. My nurse will be in momentarily."

Moments later, I am flat on my back, electrodes attached to my breasts, neck, and arms, staring at the fluorescent lights on the ceiling while her poker-faced nurse stands watching the machine spit out the paper that graphs the state of my heart. Minutes later, she deftly removes each of the electrodes and informs me that I am free to get dressed. I hop off the table, pull on my turtleneck, run a brush through my hair, and leave without even bothering to stop at the desk to make my next appointment. For the time being, the medicine will take care of things. It is, after all, only blood pressure, not something that requires hospitalization or surgery, I assure myself. Besides, I need to be on the road in an hour, and I still have to pack and say goodbye to my husband.

"HOW DID IT GO?" he asks, peering over the top of his newspaper.

"Oh, not bad," I answer casually as I hurry toward the bedroom. "I still have the blood pressure issue, but it's nothing that drugs won't rectify. I have to have a stress test when I get back and maybe see a cardiologist. Her whole response was a little over the top if you ask me."

"Actually, I don't think so." His stern voice stops me in midstep. "You're a runaway train, Joan—you never stop, you never say no. You drive here, fly there, all to have another damn best-seller. You've become nothing more than a publicity whore. Whatever happened to being present, living the simple life, knowing the moments—your lines, not mine," he says, sounding very much like Ro and Susan. "I'm glad you've been caught. It's long overdue. The question is, do you have enough self-respect to listen?" And with that, he tosses his newspaper in the trash, gives me a salute of sorts, and walks out the door.

How dare he leave me on such a note? It's as if everyone thinks I enjoy the pace of my life. And besides, what is he doing to help our cause? Ever since he retired, all he does is play golf and volunteer for a variety of local political committees. I know those are activities he never had time for before, but they don't relieve me of any of the pressure I feel to pay the bills and grow our savings. I rush off to the bedroom to stuff toiletries, makeup, and a warm-up suit into my overnight bag. The more I think about his abrupt dismissal, the more furious I become. Why does my marriage seem harder now than before? I suppose it has to do with the old adage about retirement: "Twice as much husband for half as much money." Besides which, his schedule is totally erratic. One day he might be playing golf and going to a town meeting, totally unavailable to me, and the next three days he's just hanging around. I never know what to expect from him, and because he's made it clear that he values his newfound freedom, I haven't dared to ask. Whatever. These issues can't possibly be resolved in haste. I scribble a note with my whereabouts and bolt—glad for the escape hatch.

2

Counterfeit Destinations

Early October

Be careful what you ask for, you just might get it.

—Anonymous

Despite the frantic pace of traveling, I have to admit I enjoy these quick road trips. Alone, I can spend a few hours free-associating, which always offers form and forgiveness to any impending madness. On the road, I don't have to explain my every move, and I escape the pressures that dog my everyday life. I know I've been swept away and enslaved by every idea or person who has rapped at my door the past couple of years. Once again, being all things to all people has caught up with me. So for now, I will play the nomad, a role I perfected as the daughter of a man whose company transferred him every two years. Movement is energizing. Besides, you only have to get minimally involved when you travel, dipping in and out of places and people's lives.

I am on the highway for less than a half hour when a gentle rainfall begins, bringing with it a dense fog that erases the clarity of the scrub pine woods and bogs that dot this seaside landscape. There is nothing left to distract me, so I find myself drifting backward, wondering if I can pinpoint the very moment everything in my life got so very far off track.

It isn't just my newfound career that is causing all the trouble, although I fully admit I've been dazzled by success. Once I felt the rush that comes with some level of notoriety,

I became addicted to all the accompanying "jewels"—money, recognition, talking to Oprah, having a vocation. But there have also been the effects of a burgeoning family—becoming a mother-in-law, a grandmother, caretaker of my aging mother, and most unfamiliar, the mother of married sons, both of whom are spread very thin in their own lives so that remaining close to them often feels almost impossible.

The enormity of the family web and my involvement in it was most apparent last summer, when I frequently set the dinner table for seventeen rather than seven—high chairs and wheelchairs included on any given night. Where once there were just my husband and boys, now there are spouses and children, assorted uncles, aunts, and cousins, my mother, and frequently a stray or two. And who is left to organize it all? Not the ones who are old and tired, and not the young mothers with babes in arms. Me! As wonderful as it is that so much flows through a woman's life, none of us can help but end up on empty. I laugh at how naïve I was to think years ago that running away would calm my chaos. In isolation it had been so easy. But it has been much harder than I ever contemplated to return, not least of all because I can't seem to keep all the strands of my life distinct. They always seem to be knotted around one another.

I'm reminded of a recent beach walk during which I came across a lobster trap, washed up onshore, bound in fishing line, but still connected to its buoy. I couldn't help thinking how much I am like that trap—empty of my catch, tangled and broken. I have buoyed many, but the effort has bent me out of shape. And without knowing it, I've become what I insisted I would never be—an invisible sustainer, that person who attempts to keep everyone else afloat without ever herself being buoyed. What, I want to know, is the answer? We women are never able to completely extricate ourselves from the family business, and most of us wouldn't want to. Still, one would think that our days should be less harried once everyone has been launched from the nest. But mine certainly aren't.

Much of the time my work life is the one place I feel a measure of control and peace. The real problem, though, is that I can't stop trying to top myself professionally. No accomplishment or accolade is ever enough, because deep down inside, I am still the unknown author with a manuscript that has been rejected twenty-seven times. It seems that I have been the last to accept my own good fortune, or to believe that I could sustain it. So I keep working furiously, trying to make each project better than the last one. In the end I am left only with myself, my work, and the melancholia that accompanies such single-minded focus, all the while presenting myself in public as the calm and peaceful reinvented woman who knows her moments and has clear intentions. But in truth, when I am off duty, my life is helter-skelter, mostly because of the effort required to maintain both the façade and my own ability to keep going. My emotional skin has thickened over time and so, it seems, have my arteries. I've been going full speed for so long, and now my body has finally submitted its bill.

I peddled my first book to agents and publishers for

three years. Disappointed but undaunted by each rejection, I repeatedly went back to the drawing board—tweaking, reworking, and smoothing out the story. Seeing the book in print became a full-fledged crusade fueled by my determination to prove the value of the year alone that it was about. When the manuscript finally found a home, I simply transferred all that energy and effort into making it succeed. I couldn't imagine stopping the push. Even when others backed down or moved on to other projects, I kept going. It never occurred to me that I shouldn't be working so hard or all on my own. What's more, I truly believed I had something to say to help women who, like me, had spent the better part of their lives dutifully playing the roles of daughter, wife, mother, worker without ever asking, "What's in it for me?"

As if it were yesterday, I remember standing in Union Station, Washington, D.C., having just completed my last radio interview, a fifteen-minute segment on NPR. Bob Edwards had thrown me some curveballs that I wished I had answered in a pithier manner. Still, it had been a good couple of days of hawking my book, and I felt privileged to have a tour. With half an hour to spare before my train ride home, I headed for a pay phone and called my agent.

"Liv, it's me," I said over the drone of a well-modulated voice announcing the arrivals and departures of several trains. "I just thought I'd give you an update and see what's next before I head home."

"Not much," she answered, her bland tone spelling trouble. "The news is they aren't going to publish a paperback edition."

"What?" I responded, never having thought about the next step.

"Joan, I know you are passionate about your subject," she continued, trying now to sound encouraging, "but I suggest you cut your losses and get on to something else."

"You must be joking," I gasped.

"No, I'm not. You've lost your 'in-house' support. No matter how hard you plead your case, the decision has been made. Don't take it personally. It's purely a bottom-line business thing."

Three books later, I understand more about the business of publishing, but at the time, all I knew was that I still needed to reach thousands of other women.

"Well, thanks for the news," I said weakly. "They've just called my train, and I've got to go." The raw emptiness of this sudden change in momentum left me tired and confused. I gathered up my belongings and headed for Track 6. In minutes the train roared in, lengthening down the track before it came to a stop at the platform. I pushed past several people, managed to find a seat in the quiet car, and plopped down. As the train crept out of the station, I leaned my head back and let the gentle sway rock me to sleep.

Several hours later, I awakened refreshed and with my sense of determination renewed. There has always been a part of me that is blessedly outlaw, that pushes onward and goes her own way, especially when she has been prematurely stopped. I reached for the pin on my lapel—a gold and silver fisherwoman given to me by a friend who said I was to become a "fisher of women." Just as the Little Engine That

Could, I would keep myself going with a simple mantra—*I think I can, I think I can*—in-house support or not.

When the conductor announced New Haven, I remembered a clever publicist who had an office there. She called herself the Book Doctor and specialized in creating bestsellers. As the train pulled out of the station, I made a silent pledge to call her as soon as I got home. A glass of wine seemed like a good idea, so I headed to the club car and ordered a Chardonnay. By the time I got off in Providence, I was utterly buoyant and back in my game.

That was the good news. I picked myself up and almost single-handedly fought for my book to stay in the spotlight. The bad news was that I couldn't be out there enough— promoting and pushing, leaving no stone unturned, speaking to any group that would listen, visiting bookstore after bookstore, compulsively checking the Amazon rankings and totaling up sales figures. Somehow, now that I felt spurned by the support team I had counted on, my career became more about proving myself to others than about living my own message concerning the value of a simple life. Almost overnight, the thrill of the challenge became more to me than the very wisdom my book espoused. Business, speed, working on new proposals, all the craziness became my nourishment. Not only a minor celebrity but also a workaholic was born. Now, ten years later, I am finally experiencing the toll.

A Mack truck passes me on the left, splashing a sea of water across the windshield as I grip the steering wheel and am shocked back into the present. When I've stabilized the car, as well as my nerves, I sense that there is something strangely familiar about this journey. I am heading south on 95, somewhere in Rhode Island, following in reverse the exact route I took ten years ago when I ran away from a marriage gone stale and a life on empty. What a difference a decade makes—or does it? The marriage has been mended, and my life is no longer on empty. But I am no less confused, my life no more balanced, and I am literally backtracking—driving in the very direction from which I ran.

I SEE THE SIGN for my exit and pull off the highway. On cue my stomach churns as it does before any performance. I've often wondered why I continually put myself in situations that make me so anxious. The answer is easy—to stay in the game and grasp one more brass ring.

The little town of Madison, Connecticut—one of those New England villages where all of the buildings are circa 1810 and the storefronts boast signs with words such as *Spirits, Mercantile,* and *Medicinal*—helps quell my nerves. At one end of town is a general store and at the other, a five-and-dime with an old-fashioned soda fountain. I spot a parking place right in front of the bookstore and pull in to see R. J. Julia's window display designed around a beach chair, umbrella, sand pails, shells, and of course, piles and piles of my books. I run a brush through my hair, apply lipstick, take a deep breath, shake the heaviness of my thoughts, and head for the door.

A small bell rings, heralding my entrance, and a clerk gives me an easy smile. I walk briskly through the store, barely glancing at the exposed brick walls, mahogany floor-to-ceiling bookcases, and antique tables displaying the latest fall books. I want to remain inconspicuous as long as possible, so I head for the reading room, where I can hide in an overstuffed chair and rough out a basic outline for my talk. I know what I want to say—it's just that in the moment, I fear I will leave something out.

Even though I've never enjoyed public speaking, the words of my friend and mentor, Joan Erikson, always urge me on. "The most important thing is to share what you know. Be generative. Pass it on. That is what makes all the difference." Fifteen quick minutes later, the events coordinator discovers my hiding place and escorts me to the roomful of expectant women. I straighten up, pull back my shoulders, and follow her out.

There is polite applause as I head for the lectern and place my notes on the podium. Then the room becomes eerily quiet and I stare at the expectant faces, one after another, as if I could somehow pull them up here to share the responsibility for the hour to follow. It is one thing to turn a phrase in the privacy of my office and yet another to elaborate on the experience in public, and I am overwhelmed by the urge to tell the women that I am no different than they are. I, too, am full of folly and contradictions, harassed by domesticity, and not always as kind and upbeat as I will seem tonight. What's more, my wisdom comes from hours of conversation with ordinary women such as themselves who also are trying to figure out their lives. Just as I am beginning to feel the past twenty-four hours close around me

again, I see her—Denise—a woman from one of my weekends who had told me she might be there. She is beaming,
looking radiant actually, even though she has been battered
by an ugly divorce. When I catch her eye, she nods and offers me just the encouragement I need at that very moment.

"Who are we beyond the roles that we play?" I ask the
audience. "That was my question years ago, and I assume
that is your question tonight."

As the words come, I feel oddly disconnected from myself, as if an actress had inhabited my body, perfected her
lines, and happily taken to the stage to deliver them. Mean-
while, Denise keeps on nodding as if to affirm everything I
say. Before I know it, I am halfway through the speech. I finally look past Denise and see a flash of recognition in the
eyes of the other women as well. I sense a like-mindedness
and feel as though I am truly sitting at my kitchen table with
friends. It is this companionship that keeps me going. It's
all about reciprocity. So I continue.

The analyst Jean Shinoda Bolen believed that when a
woman was at the crossroads, the heroine wanted to
make her own decision whereas the nonheroine
wanted it made for her. I believe I am standing here
in front of a group of heroines—women coming of age
who no longer need someone else's permission to
move on. To the contrary, we want to gather the
threads of our experiences and recycle them into a
new and more colorful tapestry. May you all be willing
to begin again and again. You can't really know what it

is you are supposed to do next unless you depart from the mundane to refire your spirit.

At the end, their applause is a relief. It is uniquely thrilling to evoke this kind of excitement in others. Ministering to women does have its merits, I think, as I move toward a desk and the pile of books I will be inscribing.

Denise is the first in line, and I jump up to thank her for her encouragement.

"Thank you," she whispers before I can speak. "You were perfect—said everything I needed to hear tonight. And because of that I have brought with me a surprise."

I am puzzled, wondering what she might be up to. She turns dramatically and shouts, "Ta-da!"

Out from behind a bookshelf pop four or five women—the self-named Salty Sisters—a group who met at one of my weekends and have been friends ever since. "We've canceled your motel reservation," Denise says. "We'll be at Leslie's beach house for the night and we've already made your bed."

I hesitate for a moment and then recall the last line of my speech: "You can't really know what it is you are supposed to do next unless you depart from the mundane to refire your spirit."

"Why not?" I answer with a laugh. "It's about time I did something spontaneous." Besides, on occasion "it is more blessed to receive than to give," according to the late theologian William Sloane Coffin. "At least it takes more humility."

3

In the Company of Women

Early October

*The real voyage of discovery lies not in discovering
new lands, but in seeing with new eyes.*

—Marcel Proust

Several hours later, we are driving down a darkened lane, lit-
tered with broken branches and the debris from a
nor'easter that is blowing hard off the sea not a hundred
yards away. "Run," Jeanie orders, and we dart from the car
toward the back door of a tiny cottage perched on a seawall,
following the smells of smoke and damp leaves. Leslie, our
hostess, had left the bookstore early to open up the house
and get the fire going. Just as we approach, the screen door
swings open, its hinge about to come undone. And then we
are inside, where votive candles glitter and the coffee table
is laden with every imaginable kind of finger food—
artichoke dip, smoked salmon on pumpernickel, mixed
nuts, salsa and chips.

I hang my jacket on a nearby hook and look around at
the uncurtained windows, bare rafters, and whitewashed
walls. Leslie's house has a spartan look that exudes "time
out." It is especially fitting for a women's getaway, since
there are no pillows to be fluffed or guest towels to be rearranged.

On the mantel is a card with a line written by Henry
David Thoreau: "Love Your Life." It is quickly clear to me
that this is just what these women are trying to do, and they
certainly go to extremes to succeed—flying in from Texas

and Michigan, or driving from New York and New Jersey— for just a weekend some four times a year. There are no quick and easy reunions for this widely scattered group.

It always amazes me how people who are supposed to find one another somehow do. These women first met when three of them, then complete strangers, happened to be sharing a couch during the opening session of one of my weekend retreats. As an introduction, each of the thirty women gathered in the small living room explained to the group why she was there. Leslie started off by talking about how being an empty nester had made her question what was becoming of her marriage. She described the way the hours with her husband, without distraction, were making her feel less at ease with him and even slightly panicked. Suddenly, she said, she knew what it meant to feel trapped. Leslie welled up and couldn't speak, but Denise, who was sitting next to her, finished Leslie's story.

Denise was also struggling with a marriage, and although the two women had never met before, the empathy she felt for Leslie's confusion and pain became the basis of an immediate bond. The third woman, Jeanie, came from a fashionable Detroit suburb, the type of place where dinner was always served at 6:30 and the country club still required white clothes on the tennis courts. The emotion Leslie and Denise were willing to display overwhelmed her with relief. "I've lost myself, too, and I want her back," Jeanie practically shouted when it was her turn. The rest of the women in the circle began applauding, and Leslie and Denise each gave her a quick hug.

The candor that marked the beginning of that particular weekend was unique but not unfamiliar to me. Before the first evening ended, Leslie, Denise, and Jeanie had been joined by Penny, Mindy, and Kate. This group of like-minded women instantly drew comfort from the similarity of their emotional struggles. All of them were confused, angry, and afraid to take action for themselves. They gravitated toward one another and started meeting in the middle of the night, long after the day's events were finished and the other retreaters were asleep. During the day, Leslie hid in the background, Denise wept constantly, Jeanie was stern-faced and defensive, Penny was poker-faced and unrelenting, Mindy appeared to be holding a secret, and Kate acted the clown to cover up her pain. But during all their discussions behind closed doors, they found the sustenance and support they craved. Just before they left the Cape, they named themselves the Salty Sisters and vowed to keep in touch through e-mails and regular reunions. They've included me in many of their e-mail exchanges—quick early-morning rallying cries and reminders of their circle—and I have been able to see the extent to which this friendship has helped each of them gain more control over her life. The bond among these "sisters" is nothing short of extraordinary. They have become one big transition group—nutrition for one another—a safe haven where they can try out new ideas apart from societal judgment. Watching from my chair, I am amazed at how emboldened they all seem and how comfortable I feel with them. I'm among mere acquaintances and yet I feel as if I've come home late and they've held dinner for me.

"Hey, what a speech," Denise says after asking me if I want a glass of red or white. "I learn something every time I listen to you." She is more upbeat than I recall, and the change is refreshing. Still, I don't reveal that it was her broad smile that gave me the courage to make the speech, and I certainly don't let on that I wish I could inspire myself as much as I do others.

I settle into an overstuffed chair, pull an afghan across my lap, take a sip of Merlot, and savor the moment. The room is hopping. Penny and Jeanie have wandered out onto the closed-in porch to whisper and take in the angry sea that feels as though it might plow through the French doors at any moment. Leslie is carving a small ham in her tiny yet functional galley kitchen, while Denise, the only one with teenage kids, is called to her cell phone, obviously settling some domestic issue. I overhear Mindy counseling Kate, and the words quicken my heart: "Why should you under-value yourself at *this* point? You can do anything you want to if you want it enough."

Ideas and insights are being bounced around like a Ping-Pong ball during a reckless game—it is a frenetic kind of communication that comes when friends are catching up and know their time is limited. I can't get enough of their jabbering. It amazes me how when women finally get away—from phone calls, meal making, endless errands and lists—there is a lightness of being, a joie de vivre, a blossoming. The easiness of their connection is reminiscent of a women's group I formed back in New York some time ago. We gathered to reflect on Clarissa Pinkola Estés's book *Women Who*

Run with the Wolves, and we called ourselves the Wolf Broads. We spent our evenings questioning our extremes, ascertaining just why we were all so blocked, trying to set personal goals after a lifetime of worrying about the goals of others, all the while laughing through our tears. Short of howling at the moon, we behaved like wild women. But I haven't felt such camaraderie in years. Ro, Susan, and I have shared many, many secrets and emotions, and even a few crazy nights, but our times together are too few and far between. They are intent on designing their hard-won postretirement lives, while I'm still working. Perhaps that's why I am so hungry to be included in the circle before me.

"So tell me," I ask Kate and Penny, who have settled near the blazing hearth, "what exactly has happened since I saw you last?"

"Oh my, I don't know how to answer that question! I guess you could say that we are all in varying degrees of separation—in relationships, jobs, friendships," Kate answers with a laugh.

"Yeah, Joan, all this change and upheaval is your fault," Penny jabs with a smile. "You're the one who is always talking about stepping away from the familiar to revive the spirit. Well, we've taken your advice literally."

"But it is all good," Leslie adds. "I think all of us are coming home each day a whole lot happier."

By now, Mindy and Jeanie have joined us by the fire. Everyone's settled in, and the high energy that characterized our arrival has turned into a deep sense of comfort. The cottage is warm and secure.

"So, Leslie, how was the party for your parents' anniversary?" Jeanie asks.

"It was touching, especially to see them so tender with each other after all these years," she answers as her voice trails off, although she seems to have more to say. My memory of Leslie is that she divulges her secrets the least easily, much preferring the focus to be on someone else. But she's looking around the circle right now, making sure she has everyone's attention, obviously anxious to share more.

"What?" Kate asks. "Something's wrong."

Leslie fills up. "Things couldn't be worse," she continues. "You know how Steve just hasn't been there for the last couple of years? Well, not only did he not make my parents' party, but when he's not at work, he's on the computer. He even falls asleep in front of the screen."

"So? That's par for the course for most American men, wouldn't you say?" Kate says with her usual sarcasm.

"Well, I was beginning to have my suspicions about another woman. But he was never away long enough for me to make anything of it. Then I saw something on television about men being into Internet porn."

"Oh, c'mon, Steve's too straight for that," Penny says.

"You would think so," Leslie admits, getting stronger now as she continues her story. "It took me some time to find his password, but I did."

"And?" Kate says, now sitting on the edge of her seat.

"Bingo," Leslie says. "There in his bookmarks was every porn site you could imagine. It made me sick."

"Did you take that to your shrink?" Jeanie asks.

"After confronting him with something he couldn't deny, I decided to go straight to a lawyer," Leslie answers, triumphantly and teary-eyed.

"Oh my God," Penny says, leaning over to give Leslie a hug.

"It's okay," Leslie assures her. "When he explained that I had never really loved him and that the women he met online did, I was done. Actually it is a relief. The best part of it is that I can stop trying so hard. There was nothing I wouldn't do to try and please him, and I was getting nowhere. Gone are the black nighties—gone are his office parties where I had to put on my game face—gone are the denials."

"Hopefully you aren't so anxious to get out that you'll sell yourself short financially," Jeanie says, having micromanaged her own divorce and done very well by herself.

"I listened carefully to how you handled things, Jeanie, and I've found a great woman lawyer. Money is a big issue for me. If nothing else, Steve was a good provider. But so far, he's been more than agreeable."

Leslie's story is not my story, but much about it is utterly familiar. I know my instinct is more often than not to keep my mouth shut and fit in. I do it with Robin, even after forty years of marriage; I do it with my agent and other people I work with; I even do it socially with friends like Susan and Ro. It's pitiful really, that most of us don't have more gumption or that we spend years in therapy to reverse ingrained habits.

"I don't care what you say," Jeanie says, "getting out of

any relationship is rough, especially if you are the one leaving. That was my problem. Jake couldn't stand for anyone to think he was a failure. Without me literally pulling him every step of the way, I never would have gotten the divorce."

Everyone has something to add to the conversation, an anecdote about herself or a friendly piece of advice. Just as the mood lightens and a joke or two are tossed out into the circle, Mindy quietly adds her own news.

"It is also hard to drop a lover. Especially when he has a wife to turn to and you only have an empty apartment." All heads turn immediately toward her.

"You didn't!" Kate says, looking stunned.

"I did," Mindy says with a tinge of triumph in her voice. "Listening to Penny talk about her son's drug problem last time we were together helped me turn the corner. It suddenly dawned on me that I was not in love—I was addicted, addicted to the clandestine meetings and the need to win what I stupidly thought was a prize just because it wasn't mine in the first place. So I stood him up several weeks ago and stopped answering all of his phone calls."

"Here I thought I was bringing you all down with each chapter of my saga," Penny says, reaching over to take Mindy's hand. "I'm so glad my complaining benefited someone."

As I listen to the women, I am reminded all over again that so many of our roadblocks have to do with relationships. Women, in particular, seem to find comfort in becoming involved in other people's lives. The struggle is to keep a firm hold on ourselves even as we shower others with our love. What I see this group doing is using their friendship with each other as an anchor. Just tonight, they've not only comforted and cheered each other but provided a safe place to discuss whatever struggles they are enduring. Their sisterhood is like a buoy that keeps them from sinking. It is painfully obvious that these Salty Sisters—all of whom have followed my advice and walked away from lives lived strictly in the service of others—have moved past me in at least one critical way: they are part of a circle of friends that feeds their souls, enlivens their spirits, and provides a sense of balance.

"Each one teach one," I murmur.

"Huh? Where did that come from?" Kate asks.

"Albert Schweitzer, a doctor who worked in Africa. I recite it whenever I get down on myself and know that none of us can go it alone. That's what you guys are doing for each other, and it's beautiful to watch."

"You, down on yourself!" Kate says, sounding astounded.

"From time to time. Recently more than not," I confess. "I've made lots of compromises to be where I am—counterfeit journeys, I call them, when I took a shortcut in order to make quick money or gain instant fame. I could see after the fact just how I had compromised my principles. Not that I'm any different than any other woman. Most of us, from time to time, find ourselves desperate enough to betray our very selves, in a manner of speaking. Wouldn't you say?"

I gaze around at many knowing nods. "In any case, I've

been so on the run that I had gotten far away from the direction I was headed for in the first place."

"I think you are being too hard on yourself," Mindy says. "I have a quote from *A Year by the Sea* taped to my refrigerator. It is a quote of you quoting Joan Erikson: 'You must literally be willing to begin again and again . . . energy is generated in the tension, the struggle. The pull and tug is everything.' "

Her affirmation soothes me for the moment, and surrounded by these women, I feel encouraged that I will not stay stuck forever. Just for the moment the weight of my burdens lifts.

There are yawns all around. The evening seems to be winding down. I have the urge to tidy up.

"Here's to none of us stopping," I say, lifting my glass to their tenacity, perseverance, and the simple pleasure of being included. "May our journeys continue."

These women have offered me an evening of respite and a sense of encouragement to reinhabit my own life. I feel the comfort of their arms around me as I drift off to sleep.

THE NEXT MORNING, I awaken just before dawn and tiptoe toward the living room. The sea had not been visible last night, but now I'm astounded by the expanse of low-tide beach spanning out toward the horizon. At this early hour all is slate gray, sand and sky, a neutral scene as bare as an artist's newly stretched canvas. Everywhere I look there are sleeping bodies nestled on couches or air mattresses. I walk upstairs to say good-bye to Leslie, gather my coat and bag, and slip quietly out the back door.

The storm of yesterday has stripped the trees of leaves and left a clear view of the sky—an austere yet brilliantly clean scene. The Japanese place great value on chance meetings, and after last night I understand why. This brief interlude with women who aren't even close friends has more than revived my sagging spirits. The ancient Greeks believed that only through constant dialogue and honest sharing can friends reach a higher level of truth together. After last night's celebration, I am more than certain that all women need a sisterhood of some sort.

I also learned something about myself as I listened to these women talk. If I am truly honest, I have to acknowledge that the demands I am so convinced are coming from the outer world are, in fact, coming from that perpetually unfinished part of me—the pulls and tugs originating from my own ambiguity. Susan and Ro are right. I am my own worst enemy most of the time, dogged by my perfectionism, guilt, and a need to perform. Perhaps I don't have to always get to the top of the mountain. Halfway is enough. A friend of mine recently climbed Kilimanjaro and was counseled by her guide not to feel that she had to reach the summit. "The mountain will tell you when you have gone far enough," he said. Indeed, three-quarters of the way up her nose began to bleed and her breathing became labored. It was obvious that she had gone as far as she could. Have I, too, reached my limit, at least for the time being?

Bringing up and admitting to all my counterfeit journeys

makes me think so. More than ever, I am questioning the validity of all this soul searching. My efforts were genuine at first—beginning my various journeys with the best of intentions. It's just that I lacked boundaries and things got out of hand. No crime in that. Still, all the warning signals that have recently been placed before me point to the fact that I must change directions or suffer further consequences. Setting a new set of intentions (and sticking to them) is the way to start—get an office away from home where my time will be better respected by those who tend to interrupt my space, take longer beach walks, maybe even train for the bicycle race from one end of the Cape to the other. "Believing in yourself isn't everything," Joan Erikson would say, "but you can't make a difference unless you do."

I slap the steering wheel with a new sense of determination and cheer myself onward, racing down the highway a bit too fast, but on this barren road, and at this early hour, who cares? I open the window and let the cool fall air blow my hair in a million directions. For the moment, I feel exhilarated, like Thelma and Louise only without the death wish. Totally in my own crazy world, I zoom through an underpass and catch sight of a state trooper tucked behind the brush. I remove my foot from the gas pedal and pray that he is simply having a coffee break. But seconds later, I hear the unmistakable siren, spot the flashing lights in my rearview mirror, and reluctantly pull onto the shoulder. He struts toward my little Camry and without preamble demands to see my license and registration.

I hand him both and watch as his eyes dart from my

picture to my face and back again. "Be right back," he says gruffly and marches off. I lean back against the headrest and chastise myself for being so cavalier. "Little man / (in a hurry / full of an important worry) / halt stop forget, relax," E. E. Cummings wrote, obviously just for me.

Okay. Okay! I've been caught, again. I wonder how much it will cost me. I look at the clock—it is 7:30. I've been sitting here for ten minutes. What is taking so long? I check the rearview mirror and see that he's on the phone. Oh, great! I bet I forgot to renew my driver's license or something like that. They put you in jail for that—it happened to my son on one of his late-night drives to the Cape several summers ago. I take a few more deep breaths and hum that Simon and Garfunkel tune about slowing down until the cop finally taps on my window.

"You're off the hook this time," he says as I silently sigh. "I'm only giving you a warning, since you're out of state. But we've got you on record in our computer. It's turning out to be a nice day, lady. Why don't you slow down and smell the roses?" And with that little bit of uninvited advice he is gone. I breathe a sigh of relief, turn on the ignition, ease off the shoulder and onto the highway, gaining speed but only until I am back up to sixty-five, where I remind myself to remain until safely home.

I wonder what the women back in Connecticut are up to, or if they are even awake. They had several plans for the day, including an exercise I had suggested—that they write their obituaries to mark the end of the first half of their lives—noting to whom they were related, what they'd accomplished, their passions and hobbies. The objective is to account for their time up until now so that they can mark it, see its significance, and then bid farewell to that which they were, in order to give birth to that which they might still become. I muse over what I might say about myself.

Joan Anderson, 1943–2006: As a daughter of an oil company executive, she spent her childhood moving from town to town throughout the Northeast, learning the fine art of adaptability—to become what she needed to be in order to fit into each new setting. She was sent away to a women's college, where she resisted playing bridge, smoking cigarettes, and finding someone to marry. After two years, she went on to Yale Drama School, where she oftentimes lost herself in the characters she was portraying—finding it easier to be someone other than herself. She met a fellow actor, and they sensed they couldn't live without each other. But alas, a career in the theater would not put food on the table—so the two lovers, children of the Kennedy era, ran off to East Africa to work in the bush for three years. Once back in the States, her focus turned to her husband's career and supporting a burgeoning family. The next twenty-five years involved keeping the home fires burning and raising money for school tuitions. But all this doing for others finally took its toll, and she ran away from home when it was convenient for the rest of the family. Her greatest epiphany during her year by the sea became a powerful message to women worldwide—that we are all as unfinished as the shoreline along the beach.

I laugh out loud at the thought of my own mortality and then have a sudden sense of gratitude that there is plenty of time, God willing, for additional maturity to blossom. Someone asked Robert Frost toward the end of his life if he had hope for the future; I was so taken by his answer that I memorized it: "Yes," he replied, "and even for the past . . . that it will turn out to have been all right for what it was— something I can accept—mistakes made by the self I had to be or was not able to be."

No question, life is a constant metamorphosis, especially for us women whose lives are partly controlled by the changing powers of our bodies. It was Clarissa Pinkola Estés who suggested that all women experience phases that come every seven years and change us emotionally, spiritually, and physically. The first seven, we are filled with wonder. From seven to fourteen, we are hormonal; from fourteen to twenty-one, we become sexual; from twenty-one to twenty-eight, we experience the desire to procreate, after which our time is consumed with mothering and putting others first; at thirty-five, however, we begin to wake up and look beyond such a limited existence; between forty-two and forty-nine, menopause approaches; from forty-nine to fifty-six, we desire to live without rules and go away until finally we have the chance to find our individual reason for being. It is after that that we truly become who we are—"the watchwoman," I call her.

Just now as I envision a watchwoman, I see someone noble, most probably with graying hair, whose knowledge comes from the time she has spent in the trenches of life. Her steps are deliberate, and her demeanor speaks volumes about what it means to be present as well as vitally involved. Most important, her illusions have long since been discarded and she accepts what she knows to be true for herself.

I let my shoulders drop and my mind relax; then I reach for the cell phone to alert my husband as to when I'll be home. It is so easy to reach out to those I love after I have been replenished in mind and spirit! Pitiful, actually, how little it takes for a woman to be renewed. But alas, he doesn't answer the phone, so I dial my mother's number. It will be nice to get our catch-up chat out of the way early in the day, but she doesn't answer either. With a careless shrug, I settle in to the drive and the chance to enjoy some quiet time alone with the pastoral views that Rhode Island offers—countryside dotted with freshly baled hay, cattle grazing on the hillsides, and the last of the fall foliage coloring the forests on each side of the road. Whatever peace I have lies in the natural world.

4

Detour

Early October

A good traveler has no fixed plans
and is not intent on arriving.

—Tao Te Ching

"Hi, honey, I'm home," I shout as I dump my book bag and luggage in the front hall and peer into the living room, where my husband always sits. But his chair is empty. I try once more, this time calling up the cold stairwell. "Hey, Robin, it's me, your wife!" Still, no answer. Though disappointed by the lack of homecoming, I'm not surprised. Comings and goings are not things Robin would choose to make something of on his own. I am the one who turns ordinary days into celebrations. This difference used to upset me—I used to feel overlooked or underappreciated. At least I've grown past that particular neediness. I head for the kitchen to make a cup of tea and see a scribbled note tacked to the cupboard.

Your mother's been rushed to the hospital.
I've gone to Hyannis. Come as soon as you can.

Me

Oh my God! Now what? My heart begins to pound and my stomach tightens. She was quite chipper just thirty-two hours ago. I grab the car keys and head back out, trying to minimize the possible severity of this emergency. After all, my mother has given us more than one opportunity to practice her passing.

There was surgery for a parathyroid tumor, the implantation of a pacemaker, and numerous ambulance trips to the emergency room after fainting because of hypoglycemia. She's recovered from each of these events, sometimes so quickly that I can't help but wonder if there isn't a small element of drama involved, as if these health crises offer her an excitement that otherwise eludes her at this stage of the game. I remember a trip last year to D.C. for my aunt's funeral. We had bought the plane tickets, gotten her packed, arranged for door-to-door delivery both to the airport and to our final destination, and Robin and I were her escorts! She seemed eager to go, if for no other reason than to see her brother. But halfway to the airport she became restless and soon asked for the car windows to be opened. "Joan, I don't feel well," she announced when we arrived at the airport. Nothing we did helped, and we were forced to return home. The next day she had no recollection of what had happened. Such is life with aging parents—one moment they are with it and the next they are not.

Still, each moment is a warning or foreshadowing—a sharp reminder that one of these times will mark the end. So I put a little extra pressure on the gas pedal and speed on. "Don't die, Mommy, please don't die." All my wishing that one day she would just slip away has now turned to panic. I remember a friend who lost her mother telling me to be sure and kiss mine every time I saw her. "Don't forget to smell her, too," she would add. I regret not doing either before this last trip. I was in such a rush to get away from everyone's criticism that I simply fled.

It is with these jumbled thoughts that I swing into the hospital parking lot, ditch the car in the first available space, and rush to find my husband. "How is she?" I ask without so much as a hug or hello.

"The doctor is with her now," he answers cryptically.

"What happened?"

"Got me. One of the neighbors called to say he'd found her on the floor, writhing in pain. I guess her abdomen is swollen like a basketball."

"Oh, God!" I gasp, feeling remorse that I didn't insist more forcefully that she keep the companion I had hired for her. "What do you think it is?"

"Who knows? She refused all the tests ordered by that gastro guy in Boston—didn't want to pay for them, remember?" he says, a tinge of sarcasm mixed with exasperation in his voice. "Look, there's no point in speculating," he goes on and leads me to a quiet corner away from the other people, all in varying forms of distress. "We'll know soon enough. You've got to relax. This isn't the first time we've been here and I'm sure it won't be the last."

His agitation irritates me, although on some level I understand. A good deal of it stems from the lack of freedom we feel because of our responsibilities to my mother. We'd always planned to do some serious traveling once he retired—to come and go as we pleased. But with my mother's increasing ill health, our dreams have been postponed indefinitely. For the most part, Robin's been a good sport. He plays the gallant son-in-law when my mother joins us for dinner, an increasingly frequent event, oversees her finances, handles the upkeep of her house, pays for the extra hotel room when she travels with us, and often takes her to the movies when I'm away. But recently he's been more resistant, locking the door during the day just in case she drops by. Everyone has his limits, I suppose.

So, we sit—passing time, helpless to do anything but wait. Waiting involves letting go, giving up control, and in this case, saying a prayer or two that the crisis will pass. The problem is I can't seem to settle down. I am anxious about what is happening behind the curtains and doors, and I am fearful about my mother's diagnosis. But if truth be told, I'm also a little frustrated. Just when I was ready to take the advice of my friends and family and put myself in low gear, I've run into another detour. Granted, my mother could be dying! It is only right that everything should stop, but I am anxious not to lose the sense of possibility and hope I gained in Connecticut.

Several hours and many cups of coffee later, the doctor approaches. He is a handsome, older man with a kindly face. "Your mother will be fine," he says. "We've untwisted her colon, which was certainly obstructing any movement, but she will need an operation. Without surgical repair, the problem will reoccur. It'll take a couple of days to prepare her," he continues. "You can see her now if you like."

We follow him to my mother's cubicle, where she lies on a narrow gurney looking shy and somewhat terrified, surrounded by interns and nurses taking blood and inserting various tubes. The skin on her face looks like parchment. I take her hand and bend down to give her a kiss, and the strength of her grip tells me how grateful she is that we are there. "You'll be all right," I say, hoping to assuage any anxiety—hers and mine.

"I know, dear," she says, "and what a nice doctor, don't you think? Did you notice his shoes? He's wearing clogs. Imagine!" Her silly remarks bring momentary relief, and Robin and I both laugh. When the busy staff ask us to step out into the hallway, Robin seizes the chance to leave.

"Granny, you're in good hands now. I think it's best if Joan and I head home now," he says to my mother without so much as thinking to consult me. "We'll be back first thing in the morning." I know he has an aversion to hospitals and his manner is often unintentionally gruff, but I have long felt that the elderly, especially if they are one's parents, deserve and need an advocate when they're in a strange environment. Leaving her like this before she's even been assigned a room seems uncaring—even cruel. Nonetheless, he gives her a wave and then takes my arm to usher me out. Once in the parking lot, he is the first one to talk. "Have you noticed that every time you go away she either takes to bed or is rushed to the hospital? Kind of psychosomatic if you ask me."

He isn't a mean person and I know he's tired, but can't he be more sensitive to my conflict? I at least wanted to see her to her room before taking off. "Certainly you aren't suggesting that this illness isn't real, are you? They don't readily cut open ninety-year-olds."

Fortunately we are driving separate cars, so this little debate doesn't go any further. But it has fed the flames of a struggle I'm having with myself. Being "on call" for my mother as I have been for the past ten years has become more than tiresome. It all began after my father's death, when I mistakenly thought I could fill the void left by his passing and assuage my mother's pain. So as our boys left home I took on the caretaking of another child—my mother. With her various faculties beginning to fail—incontinence, worsening hearing, fading sight, and the worst, impending senility—this role has taken on new proportions.

Now just looking at my once chic mother day after day depresses me. Her complexion has become gray, her eyes dull, her hair matted, her gait unsteady. The woman who always wore color-coordinated clothes with matching shoes and jewelry has all but disappeared, and in her place is an old woman who wears the same warm-up suit day after day and waits to be entertained by me. If truth be told, I find it harder to take care of my elderly mother than I do my rambunctious grandchildren, who although exhausting to be around, have full lives ahead of them and are fun to watch.

Though difficult, my relationship with my mother is familiar. She herself took care of both her parents and my father's mother and aunt. I must have assumed that I had no choice but to do the same. Still, most women in my mother's generation didn't have careers, as I and so many of my peers do. See, I am right back where I started three days ago— overwhelmed by my full plate, entangled in familial obligations.

It was only after meeting Joan Erikson that I began to

see the depth of my instinct for caretaking. We were comparing each other's strengths when she volunteered that I had the strength of compassion. I was, of course, utterly flattered—who wouldn't want to be seen as compassionate? Joan went on to explain that I must have play-acted a lot as a child, and in doing so, I was made to figure out what was going on in other people's lives so that I could better relate to them. "So now," she informed me, "as an adult, you are quite adept at relating deeply to others. It's remarkable how well you understand the plight of your elders. But I wonder, dear, if you don't sometimes feel so much for other people that you can't feel for yourself."

As the years have marched on I see the nemesis I've created by being so compassionate—intertwining myself with the lives of others much more than was necessary—creating their need for me so that I can keep on doing what I do best. My mother made me dependent on her and I have now made her dependent on me. But what to do about it?

My brother made it clear some years back that he had no intention of parenting his parents. So far it's been easy for him to stick by that declaration. After all, he's male and lives a good two thousand miles away, in the state of Utah. He would like to think he is contributing by calling Mom every week, visiting in the summer, and sending care packages, but the day-to-day care falls to me. After each emergency, Robin renews his campaign to sign her up for assisted living. She refuses, of course, and I must say I haven't been pushing. At times, the prospect of having my mother in an institution feels like I'd be giving up and putting her out to pasture. I remember the pit in my stomach each time I sent the boys to overnight camp knowing they'd be homesick. Yet, the wedge that is occurring between Robin and me must be addressed. Last time we argued about my self-imposed role of caregiver, Robin made an interesting point. "Pills and pacemakers have changed the natural course of things," he said. "What I want to know is, what are we gaining in the process?"

He's right. This game is getting old, and when I am not in the middle of a crisis, I often think about the fact that our elders, my mother included, have had their turn—a lifetime of children, grandchildren, and great-grandchildren. Aren't I entitled to the same? I'm ashamed to admit that I've even fantasized about being part of the Eskimo culture, where, when it is time and old people have outlived their natural life span, they build them an igloo and leave them alone.

What I see now is that I'm cheating myself of my turn. If I don't step up to the plate soon, I will lose my time at bat altogether. The clock is ticking. If any of us knew precisely the day we were going to die, would we live differently? Knowing the moments, valuing them, using them wisely is precisely what I set out to do that year I spent alone. How do I get back to that deliberateness? The answer is right in front of me—I seize the moment.

Before going home, I stop at my favorite Italian market and pick up the ingredients to make a vegetable pasta dinner—peppers, tomatoes, mushrooms, garlic, zucchini, freshly shaved Parmesan cheese, a huge loaf of bread, and an overpriced bottle of Chianti. Back in the car, I call Robin.

"Hey, it's me. How about an Italian dinner tonight?"

"I was going to take you out, sweetie."

"Well, putting my feet up and sitting by the fire feels better to me. I just stopped at Ferretti's and picked up some stuff."

"If it sounds good to you, it sounds good to me," he says, his voice unusually warm.

By the time I walk in the door, he has a fire crackling and even some candles lit. "I think I'm suffering from elderly burnout," I murmur, as I bury my head into his chest.

"Good to hear that," he says as he takes the bag of groceries out of my hands. I lean back against the kitchen counter and watch him unpack the bag.

"When do you feel our life will be normal again?" I ask. "You know, not exceptional, not inspirational, just normal."

"What's normal?" he quips. "We're made to work with the hand we're dealt."

As usual, his answer is short and direct, and I'm left to ponder his thought.

"What's this?" I ask, noticing a book that is all but prominently displayed on the counter: *Caregivers in Decline*, an ominous title to say the least.

"Hits the mark for our present situation, don't you think?" Robin says, while handing me a glass of wine. "We don't need to talk about it tonight, but there are some scary statistics that might bring you to attention where your mother is concerned. Look, Joan, I don't want to be hard on you—your heart is in the right place, and besides, you gave many years to my parents. It's just that now there appears to be no end to it."

"I know," I say while putting on my apron and starting to chop vegetables. Life certainly doesn't unfold in any predictable way—it moves in loops and switchbacks. And my life can't stop just because my mother is ill. I can and will be her advocate, but I must remain compassionate to myself. There is a counterpoint to everything—for each goal, a loss; for every placement, a displacement; for every season, a passing one. Nothing just stops. But tonight I am determined to take hold of the steering wheel and drive onto a road of my own choosing. There is something thrilling about an almost empty house.

5

Proceed with Caution

Early December

Traveling is not just seeing the new;
it is also leaving behind. Not just opening doors;
also closing them, never to return.
But the place you have left forever is always there
for you to see, whenever you shut your eyes.

—*Jan Myrdal*

'Tis the season to be jolly, or so the familiar carol goes, yet I'm hardly feeling festive. I've gone to great pains to tell myself that it doesn't matter if the family is together for the holiday, but I find it still does. My mother's recuperation from surgery has prevented us from visiting either of our sons. She's out of the hospital and back in her house with help but not completely recovered. I couldn't possibly, in good conscience, leave her alone this Christmas.

The other day I unpacked a box of old Christmas books that we get out each year, and I began leafing through my favorite, *Why the Chimes Rang*. Although a picture book for children, it relays a message that I needed to hear—a story about two brothers who, while walking to church on Christmas Eve, come upon an elderly lady who has fallen in the snow. The older brother feels compelled to stay behind and comfort her, but he sends his brother on to the service with a pouch of coins they had saved, in hopes that their gift for the Christ child will make the chimes ring—something that hasn't happened for years.

Alas, when the boy arrives on the cathedral steps, the service is over and the chimes are silent. Nonetheless, the young boy makes his way to the altar, kneels down, and places his small offering next to grander ones of gold, jewels, precious works of art. Just as he does, the organ stops and everyone gathered inside listens intently to the unexpected sound—a gentle pealing at first, and then a larger, bolder ringing as the giant bells flood the cathedral in glorious melody. The chimes ring once again, all because of the unassuming but determined gift of two young boys.

I closed the book and knew where I belonged this Christmas. For all of its frivolity, decorations, sentimentality as well as good cheer, Christmas is a time of selflessness. My mother deserves our companionship this year—there will be other years with children and grandchildren. For now I must have faith that the packages have been shipped and our gifts will make the chimes ring in the hearts of our grandchildren.

I have to admit that part of me is relieved not to be taking a long flight in the busiest of seasons only to feel like a guest who has dropped in on someone else's holiday. We've spent myriad Christmases trying to fit into the kids' busy schedules by lugging expensive, thoughtful gifts across the country and orchestrating the making of gingerbread houses or the stringing of popcorn just to have an influence on the grandchildren's sense of the holiday. But, if truth be told, most of the time I feel as though I'm stretching far to make my mark. Other times, I feel as if I am at the center of a wild game of Twister, my feet and hands all planted in different circles. Besides, there is usually more tension than joy at our family get-togethers; this year will be peaceful at least. I'm doing just what the doctor ordered a few months back—having a self-imposed shutdown—forgoing any agenda in order to be still.

Still, I feel like Scrooge and want to bark "humbug" at everyone around me. I'm moved to decorate the house one minute and not be bothered the next. We did go to the lighting of the town Christmas tree, and I unpacked our homemade crèche, both of which made me miss the kids all the more. The one event I've refused to cancel is my wreath party—a gathering of friends who come together to sip wine as they create decorations for their front doors—a tradition I've created just for me.

Since that very party is today, Robin has insisted that we get the twinkle lights up on our picket fence. "C'mon, sweetie, we've got to do something seasonal," he says, urging me off the couch and away from *The New York Times*. It is so uncharacteristic of him to think of pushing the holiday spirit. Maybe he's feeling the empty nest as much as I am.

"You know it is natural to feel sad," he says reassuringly as he puts his arm around me and we head for the shed to find the lights. "For twenty years, we created rituals, never thinking it would all come to a grinding halt. We knew that one day we'd have to share the kids with other families, but I, for one, never dreamed that would mean an end to family Christmas gatherings altogether. Hell, I feel as if all that tradition just evaporated."

I smile and snuggle into the crook of his arm. He has cut right to the heart of my conflict. What was the point of all those years of effort? What is lasting anymore? And did my mother or Robin's ever feel this way when we were starting our own family traditions?

It was apparent early on that both our boys were determined to have lives of their own as they ran here and there—chasing girls, dreams, adventures—the farther away the better, it seemed. "You know, it's all your fault," I tease, as we start to untangle the lights. "You were the nomad when you were young. I guess it rubbed off on our sons."

He laughs and wraps a strand around the top of the fence.

"I've been thinking about what Kahlil Gibran wrote in *The Prophet*, that 'your children are not your children. They are the sons and daughters of Life's longing for itself.' Do you think the boys know how much we miss them?" I ask.

"To tell you the truth, I don't think they have time to think about it. Besides, they both married strong women just like you." His comment stings even though I understand that it is true.

"That business about not losing a son but gaining a daughter is hogwash, absolute hogwash," I declare. "This whole relationship with married sons feels like an amicable divorce, if you ask me."

"Don't you think that's a bit strong?"

"No, I think it's accurate—at least for right now. I never envisioned life without a one-on-one relationship with each of my children, and I can't recall when I last had so much as a moment with either of them alone. I was complaining to a friend the other day that Andy isn't dead, he's just married."

"Now, Joan, they do call."

"They call *you* when they have a problem or need money, but never me. I'm the odd woman out, no question about it," I say while weaving the lights in and out between the pickets.

I know that what I've said is not altogether true. In fact, as soon as the words leave my mouth, I have a vivid memory of my last visit to California to see Andrew, our older son, just after the birth of his third son. I hadn't been in their house for more than a few hours when I could feel the tension. It's one thing to observe your children's triumphs and joys and another to be a part of their agony—a sort of reality television show gone bad. It was so easy when the boys were young and I could kiss their hurts and bandage their wounds. But now Andy seemed overwhelmed with responsibility—not enough money, too much work—and in a weak moment he asked me what I did when things got bad. Since I didn't know what he meant by bad, I answered cautiously: "Endured."

"That's hardly helpful," he shot back.

"Well, it's the hard that makes it great," I said, smiling. "When one of your marathons gets tough, where do you take your head so you don't quit?" It was a risky analogy. Andy had been running ultra-marathons, fifty- and one-hundred-mile races, for a few years. Robin and I both felt that the physical strain was too much, not to mention the pressure it put on his daily life. With two, now three kids, a full-time job as the head of a private school, and a modern marriage in which the husband was expected to do as much around the house as the wife, Andy had to wake up at 4:30 A.M. to run his ten miles, come home to help get the kids off to school, and work all day. The weekends were even worse. On Saturdays and Sundays, his runs sometimes took six to seven hours. But he was very good and clearly determined to succeed. I followed each of his races from afar, feeling a mixture of fear and tremendous pride.

"Look, you've been on a roller coaster these past two years," I continued. "You interviewed all over the country before taking this job; you sold your house in Phoenix, moved out here to Oakland, decided to rent because you couldn't afford to buy, and now have had a third baby—hell, who do you think you are that you shouldn't crack one way or another?" I registered a sigh of relief on his face. "Pausing, taking some time, just being is my prescription for you right now, Andy."

"Yes, but my wife just had a baby."

"All the more reason to be still—be here, but be quiet. Take in what you have and take on nothing new. Give yourself the time and space to recuperate. Your wife needs that from you."

"I'll try," he said weakly.

Before I left, I said to him, "Andy, don't ever forget—no man is an island. We've finally begun to talk again. Let's keep the dialogue going. It's good for both of us. And for God's sake, answer my e-mails."

"You know, Mom, I might not."

"Why?"

"Because you happen to be one of the few persons in the world I can actually disappoint." I wasn't sure exactly how to take his comment. Although bittersweet and shocking, even, for once we were talking truth like we used to when he was growing up. As he was the firstborn and somewhat my soul mate, I suppose I longed for more of such intimate moments during this most sentimental of seasons.

"Hey, sweetie, you're falling down on the job," Robin says, snapping me out of my daze.

"Sorry," I say, though I can't remember where we were in our conversation, or what I was supposed to be doing with the lights. I generally don't help with this task because I am too busy baking or shopping or planning a meal. I think, if I am honest, that what I miss most this year is the flurry of energy and activity. I was always the producer of Christmas, and now I don't have that job anymore. Still, even when we visited the kids the past couple of holidays, they didn't give me much to do. I felt relegated to the sidelines.

"I'll tell you one thing I won't miss this Christmas." Robin cuts into my thoughts again. "Sleeping on a goddamn air mattress in someone's basement. I'm getting too old for that."

I chuckle, not only at all the times I've watched my six-foot-four husband on hands and knees trying to rouse his twisted body after a night on the floor but also at how he brings me back to reality. What am I really longing for? I ask myself.

"I'm certainly not going to miss shopping for Christmas dinner—on Christmas Eve—and then paying for everything," I offer.

Few of our get-togethers with the kids are ever cheap or free from trauma, and I always end up turning myself into a pretzel so that I don't step on anyone's toes. At Luke's, most of the trouble starts in the kitchen. According to him, I barely know how to toss a salad, let alone empty the dishwasher or put the garbage in the proper bag. I sense a certain anger toward me from time to time—a frustration that I cannot anticipate how he wants things done—whether I'm unpacking the groceries, playing on the floor with his children, strapping them into their car seats, or cleaning up the toys on the nursery floor.

I don't know quite what he wants me to be at this age. Perhaps now that he has his autonomy he thinks that he can make me what I wasn't for him all along, and that I will grow into the mother he once longed for me to be. Or perhaps this is another version of what Andy revealed to me—that I happen to be the only one right now he can resist, dismiss, or be frustrated with. It is safe for him to complain about how I make a salad or fold clothes because that won't upset the precarious equilibrium he and his wife, as young parents, have at home; besides, he's learned I won't fight back. I suppose there is an honor in here somewhere.

Another plus about not visiting this Christmas is that I don't have to worry about getting in trouble with the girls. Learning how to dance with my daughters-in-law has been the hardest adjustment I've made since the boys got married. It seems as if, without even trying, I have gotten into my share of pickles. Bestowing gifts and helping them with moves and babies never earned me the points I had expected. The latest faux pas happened when I went to Luke's to help after their second child was born. Because they were getting ready to remodel their house, I jumped right in and began reorganizing a very messy basement, inadvertently tossing away some undelivered Christmas gifts. Although good intentions abounded, I nonetheless incurred my daughter-in-law's wrath. It really wasn't about the gifts in the end—it was that I overstepped another woman's boundaries: her house, her things, her secrets even, which might have been stashed in the basement she did not ask me to clean. She took her anger out on Luke, which then left him caught between his wife and his mother. I skulked out of the house at the end of my stay and felt awful that my visit had caused trouble rather than the hoped-for peace.

"There really is no job training for being an in-law or a mother to grown children, is there?" I ask Robin.

"I suppose not," he says, intent now on finishing this immediate job. "We need another extension cord and then we're ready to go live," he says at last.

I rush off and return minutes later, actually excited. The boys and I have come to label this as Dad's Chevy Chase moment—when he plugs the cord into the master switch and voilà, magic happens. Indeed, even without the boys, the anticipation is no different. "Ta-da!" he shouts with a flourish as the lights go on and I run out onto the street to take it all in.

Minutes later, as if on cue, my friend Geri pulls into the driveway. She has always helped collect greens for the wreath party, and this year is no exception. Children or no children, Christmas is coming.

"Hi, dear," she says, opening her car door and beckoning me in. I grab my plastic bag, clippers, and gloves, and we head out for a nearby meadow where holly, rose hips, juniper berries, soft pine, and bayberry, abound. "I just love this party—gets me into the spirit."

"You know, just about everyone is coming. I'm always surprised that anyone can find the time. December is so hectic," I say.

"But we make the time. Just walking into your home and smelling all these greens we clip, the candles flickering, good munchies, and a hot toddy or two is bliss. It's about the best Christmas moment I get."

In ancient times this season was not about family get-togethers but rather about giving in to the darkness, meditating on what seeds to plant for the future, and then resting, allowing the soil of one's soul to lay fallow until it was time again to germinate. Pity that, instead of living with the customs of the ancients, we've turned Christmas into the busiest and craziest time of the year.

"So where are you going for Christmas," she asks, "Luke's or Andy's?"

"Neither."

"Why?" she gasps.

"It's my mom. She's somewhat on the mend, but we can't bring ourselves to leave her at Christmas."

"I'm sorry. It must be so hard to be torn. Our Bill keeps moving farther and farther away, but we have Jennifer right here in Boston. I guess I should consider myself awfully fortunate."

"Do you realize how much I envy you having kids within driving distance, where you can just pop in and pop out and not really intrude?" I say, as I fill a plastic bag with branches of the most vibrant blue junipers. "When we visit it feels like such a big deal, especially for my daughters-in-law, who spend days getting their houses in shape. By the time we walk in the door, they are exhausted."

"But didn't you do the same? They so want to make a good impression."

"I know, but it still means we're on formal terms. That's the part that gets me. When can we just be friends and family, where all that formality no longer matters?"

"Well, you know that the Chinese character for conflict is two women under the same roof," she says. "You told me that once and I've never forgotten it."

"It's so true, and yet I had hoped to get beyond that by now with my daughters-in-law. Shelly is forty and Susannah is thirty-eight. I have no interest in judging their lives—not that I would if I could; I just want a place in them."

We are in a thicket of wild rose hips, and I'm clipping like crazy while Geri holds open the plastic bag so I can dump them in. "In any case, I'm beginning to think that visiting kids during normal times—not Christmas or other big events—offers a more natural experience."

"Certainly time with less tension," she suggests. "So much goes into Christmas—getting everything just right for the big day."

"True, but last week I found myself crying in the grocery store at the sight of animal crackers and ribbon candy—both of which were always in the boys' stockings."

"You must have been the queen of tradition," Geri says with a laugh. "I'll bet you anything that at least one of them has put ribbon candy in his children's stockings."

Geri is right; I've been dwelling too much on what's

changed and not enough on what's lasted. Not one holiday goes by without a phone call from each of the boys with a request for a family recipe, instructions on how to boil Easter eggs, or what color the candles should be for the Advent wreath. Just last week Andy asked me to send him the actual pattern for the gingerbread house. We might not be there in person, but much of our tradition and ritual is nonetheless. I wouldn't be surprised if both Andy and Luke have their own Chevy Chase moments with lights.

Our bags are filling up—this pilgrimage on a damp and chilly day has assuaged my depression, and I suspect that my longing takes up more energy than actually being with the kids does. I have spent enough time wishing and worrying rather than just being grateful for what they have—and what we have as a result.

I wander toward a huge blue spruce, which always seems to have hundreds of pinecones underneath its branches. As I bend down to begin filling up my basket, I spot the most intricate spiderweb draped over numerous limbs, complete with dew drops glistening in the late-afternoon sun. Such meticulous creations not only fill me with awe but today remind me of the intricacies of family—how once we were manageable and small. Now with spouses, children, in-laws, and extended relatives, the web is more complicated. Still, this small marvel before me is the salve I need to buoy my holiday feelings. I may not be able to see or touch the events in my children's lives, but I know we are all connected, spun out in different directions, yet all part of the same glorious web.

6

Miles to Go

Late December

What we call the beginning is often the end.
And to make an end is to make a beginning.
The end is where we start from.

—T. S. Eliot

Lately, I have been taking too many unspoken frustrations and conflicts to bed with me. It's no wonder I'm plagued by bad dreams and often awaken in the middle of the night. Once I accept the futility of tossing and turning, I usually get up and hope that the very act of moving around will provide solutions, or at least the ability to organize my thoughts.

It is almost the New Year, and I've yet to steady my own ship. I still feel as if I am drifting from crisis to crisis. My mother is still not back to her old self. Although I am not intimately involved in her care, she does count on me for daily visits as well as the usual mother-daughter camaraderie. Plotting her future continues to be the chief source of tension between Robin and me. With no answers and plenty of questions, I creep down to the kitchen and put the kettle on to make a cup of ginger and lemon tea. As I wait for the water to boil, I can see the almost full moon through a skylight. Is that the reason for tonight's restlessness? I suspect it has just as much if not more to do with the fading year. I'm one of those strange souls who cries at the stroke of twelve on New Year's Eve, but this year I am mourning the fact that the past year is a total blur.

I take my tea into the living room, settle into the window seat, and pull a blanket that has the word BREATHE embroidered on one of its corners up around my shoulders. It was a gift from my friend Vicki, who also wanted me to slow down. When this particular blanket didn't produce the intended outcome, she gave me another one embroidered with the word PEACE. This second blanket came with a plaque that now hangs in my office: "Peace . . . it does not mean to be in a place where there is no noise, trouble, or hard work. It means to be in the midst of those things and still be calm in the heart."

I smile as I think of Vicki. She attended one of my first retreats and a few months later got the message loud and clear about slowing down, not so much from me but from a bad diagnosis. She had contracted a serious lung problem and her doctor told her that she had a choice between talking or breathing. For six months she remained absolutely silent, not speaking to anyone and limiting her exposure to people in general. Rather than resorting to a pad and pen, or a system of hand gestures, Vicki embraced silence and turned inward. She used the time to reflect on the craziness of life and ultimately found a modicum of serenity.

Before her diagnosis, she had been a self-proclaimed workaholic with no sense of an inner life. I was using Joan and Erik Erikson's Life Cycle chart during the retreat she attended, and she promptly claimed that the only strength she possessed was Hope—the first strength the Eriksons listed, which was purported to be gained during infancy. The other strengths come as we work our way up the ladder of life—qualities such as Will, Purpose, Competence, Fidelity, Love, Care, and Wisdom. I distinctly remember not only the puzzlement on her face but also the pain. She looked like a woman who felt completely left out of her own life. Despite being fifty-one years old, she claimed she lacked every one of the other seven strengths. The remainder of the weekend I frequently found her pondering the large Life Cycle chart that was hanging in our meeting room.

		STRENGTH GAINED
Infancy	Trust vs. Mistrust	Hope
Early Childhood	Autonomy vs. Shame	Will
Play Age	Initiative vs. Guilt	Purpose
School Age	Industry vs. Inferiority	Competence
Adolescence	Identity vs. Confusion	Fidelity
Young Adult	Intimacy vs. Isolation	Love
Adulthood	Generativity vs. Stagnation	Care
Old Age	Integrity vs. Despair	Wisdom

Vicki was driven to understand the Eriksons' idea that as an individual works through one adversity after another, she gains one strength after another. Once clued in to what was missing in her life, Vicki made a silent pledge to retreat again and again, each time working to acquire the various strengths.

Although frightening and unsought, her medically imposed silence forced her to stick to her vow—it took away any chance she might otherwise have had to slip back into old habits and ways of living and relating. When she could talk again, she continued to work hard to claim solitude as a priority, stepping aside frequently from her once frantic life to make room for reflection.

As I take a sip of my tea and think about my friend's story, I see that she always possessed an abundance of strengths, but the entanglements that came with her chaotic life caused her to lose her sense of them. President of her own dance company, she fostered that company's growth even while going through a divorce. She was a daughter, mother, and grandmother. When forced into isolation, Vicki realized that she certainly possessed some degree of will, purpose, and competence. But when her body called for a time-out, she had the spiritual resources to go inside and hear what her heart needed to tell her. In the end, Vicki restructured her company with an eye to selling it; she rented a house for the year on a delta in Alabama; and she made plans to pursue her dream of becoming a writer.

Vicki's odyssey holds several lessons for me. Although the Eriksons' chart indicated that individuals develop certain strengths at specific passages in their lives, I'm coming to believe that once a person has gained a strength, she doesn't simply move on to the next one. She is meant to build on any previously acquired strengths again and again—a sort of recycling of the life cycles. Hope, for instance, is not acquired or available only when we are young. As one brass ring after another appears, we are meant to be hopeful enough to reach out again and again, thus strengthening our strengths. Perhaps that's what Joan Erikson meant when she insisted that "life is a progression—that it is important to be aware and ready to greet the next passage."

Each year around this time, I take stock of the past twelve months, listing all the events and moments I can recall and then identifying them as exhilarating, exhausting, or experiences shared with my husband. But tonight I can do better. It's been ten years since I came to the Cape—a decade that has made such a difference. What has transpired? Who was I back then? What have I actually accomplished? What has been left undone? If as Shakespeare wrote, "what's past is prologue," perhaps answering these questions will give me a glimpse of the remaining plot. Like Vicki, I need to look back and see just what strengths I've gained but also lost sight of in all the rushing and doing and caretaking. It was Joan Erikson who proposed that "a full life is about self-cultivation. We owe it to ourselves to create something out of nothing." According to her, it is simply a waste of time to dwell on such things as what your mother did to you—rather, she would ask, what will you do for yourself?

I reach for a yellow legal pad and pen and start scribbling, thinking back to who I was ten years ago, listening for my life, recalling the key moments and in so doing realizing that nothing that happened was commonplace. Then I was a middle-aged woman co-existing with a husband in an empty house, getting to know him in a new way as we lived together day and night, attempting to reconfigure the meaning of family after the fact, writing my story, hoping to get it published. Aside from looking in the mirror at newly emerging crow's-feet and a white hairline, it is hard to pinpoint the moment of actual metamorphosis. Humans change subtly compared, for instance, with butterflies, which burst into full glory from their chrysalises.

As I recall coming to the Cape—the rash decision and radical departure—I see how this past decade began in crisis, a time when I was so disgruntled that I ran away to live by myself. The strength I regained by being close to nature and living on my own was *hope*, a quality I had lost when the intensity of raising a family got the best of me.

At the beginning of the decade I felt shame—shame that I couldn't work it out with my husband, shame that I had to run and hide, shame that I couldn't at least appear perfect like the suburban neighbors I had left behind. But as I learned to survive alone and even enjoy my own company, I felt the joy of autonomy for the first time and as a result was gifted with a resurgence of *will*.

Being independent, making my way without calling for help, changed how I would be for the rest of my life. Having been taught to be compliant and dependent, I now had to learn the rules that go with being separate. The first rule was the need for more financial independence—knowing that I could provide for myself with or without a husband. I had to find a job, any kind of job, and not worry how my choice might look to others. A good day's work at the fish market for a good day's wages was all that it was about.

I did what I knew best and wrote about my experiences during my year of solitude. Although the writing was hard and getting published even harder, I no longer felt weak and inferior, as I had when I arrived on Cape Cod. The tough job of writing challenged me, made me all the more industrious, and during the long process of rejection, rewriting, and publishing, I began to feel very *competent*—not only as a writer but as a self-made person.

When the book became a success and women all over the country wrote to me to say that my words were their words, I no longer felt confused. I had unintentionally become a change agent—a woman willing to share her experience in order to help other women find themselves. Finally I felt as though I had my own identity, and with that came a feeling that I was being true to myself, or as the Eriksons labeled it, I had the strength of *fidelity*.

I was no longer isolated—to the contrary, there were too many people in my life. But one thing I gained was the respect of my husband. As we talked endlessly about who we were now, as opposed to who we had been, we grew in spirit, which allowed for a new level of intimacy. In short, I finally had *love*—not the adolescent variety I faintly remember, but something deeper and more comfortable, much like a favorite old sweater. I suppose I knew this when last Christmas he gave me a glass bowl on which he had inscribed MARRIED AND UNFINISHED—unfinished because instead of living out the rest of our lives being stagnant, we have each chosen to be more vitally involved: he in town and state politics, I through my writing and workshops, and both of us with each other.

It occurs to me that adults are always eager to applaud their children's accomplishments—walking, climbing, jumping, running, writing, and speaking—yet we hardly notice our own. We may not change so much outwardly (as growing children do), but we are evolving internally all the time. The measuring of our days becomes all the more important, if for no other reason than that we must track our progress and continue to foster our own internal and personal growth spurts. Every decade brings with it a new certainty—a time of passage—a walking through the portal to the other side. Wouldn't it be interesting if there was an actual ritual at the end of each decade that marked a woman's achievements—her crises managed, lessons mastered, attitudes and ideals changed—so that we weren't merely aging but rather honoring, ritualizing, and affirming life's progress? As I look back, this particular decade astonishes me. But the thing I am missing is being grateful that I had both the desire and the inclination to keep striving all the time. It's 4:00 A.M. and I feel as if I'm onto something. No climbing back into bed tonight.

Just now, I hear the distinct thud of the newspaper being tossed onto the front porch. I wrap myself more tightly in the blanket and step out into the early hour, lit only by the large ball of moon. The crisp air awakens me as if out of a deep sleep, and I quickly bend over to pick up the paper when I see the headline: MONOMOY JOINED TO SOUTH BEACH AND THE MAINLAND.

Rarely do I ever take notice of the news, much less be affected by it. But this morning I am both startled and intrigued, and rush back inside to settle into the window seat and devour the story about my very precious beach. It was here that I was dropped off some ten years ago to swim with the seals; where I arrange for boats to drop my weekend women to be alone, gather their thoughts, and then trek back to the lighthouse; where metaphors abound in a wild and barren landscape. Despite the development all over Cape Cod, South Beach has remained a constant—its wildness perfect for anyone who needs to lighten her load, dump excess emotional baggage, and exorcise memories of abuse, grief, fear, helplessness, loneliness, and mistrust. Now it is part of a bigger picture—joined to an island, connected by a natural bridge formed by shifting sands.

I read on, fascinated by the history of this heretofore remote island called Monomoy. Originally it had been part of the mainland, but in the 1950s a storm separated it from Chatham and it became an island. Some twenty years later another fierce winter storm split the island in two, and then thirty years later the gradually elongating Chatham beach attached itself to Monomoy, thereby making it part of the mainland again. My interest is further piqued by this anomaly, since I have just spent the night contemplating the process of change and re-creation—trading an old life for a new one. I read on, taking particular interest in an essay by local environmentalist Robert Finch.

If I've learned anything from living here, it's that the world is not geared to large answers, and certainly not to final ones. One's foundations continually shift, the sea breaks through in new places, forming new inlets, closing off old ones, running in new currents. Old species leave, new ones arrive: only the processes of creation and change remain. Those of us who live here on the Cape should know this well. All we have to do is sit still and watch the world change around us.

Suddenly I have a need to see for myself the power nature has to create such change. What better way to mark the decade past than with a pilgrimage to my original starting point—to where all my wild and salty juices were evoked—the very place where I began to rediscover my own individual self.

"Ah wilderness," Robert Finch says, "whatever we think it is, the ocean has its final say." Still, it will be a challenge to find a boat for hire at this time of year. My only chance is Hillary, a shell fisherman whose wife is a friend of mine. He hardly misses a day out on the flats. I put on the coffee and wait for dawn, feeling a newfound sense of expectancy.

7

Unfamiliar Territory

January

*We tire of just seeing. What we want is
vision to be able to name that which we see
as a manifestation of grace.*

—Marv Hiles

Days later, I am driving my car onto a road of crushed clamshells that cuts through two rows of ramshackle shacks in which the fishermen store their gear. I am headed toward a tranquil little harbor known only to those who make their living off the sea, and where Hillary insisted I arrive no later than 7:30 A.M. "I leave three or four hours before low tide to give myself a full five hours of actual digging," he explained to me on the phone. "Sets my whole week, the tide cycle does."

How coincidental, I thought as I hung up the receiver. *His days are controlled by the tide cycles and my thoughts have been about life cycles.*

After parking the car, I spot Hillary rowing out to his twenty-four-foot boat. "Be back in a couple of minutes," he calls, his voice echoing around the empty cove. Although mild for January, the air is crisp, and from the looks of the variety of bobbing vessels, there is a stiff offshore breeze.

I watch as Hillary loosens his boat from the mooring and heads toward the dock. "Hop aboard—that is, after you hand me all my stuff," he says, pointing to a pile of paraphernalia. When I worked in the fish market, I would watch the fishermen lug their gear down to the dock and onto their boats. To a novice, the work seemed soothing, an early-morning ritual no different from emptying a full, clean dishwasher as the coffee brewed. But alas, fishing is like any other profession: hard work. Just now I am learning how much Hillary's pile weighs, how slippery each piece can be, and how much work is involved simply to get under way. I stuff my desire to jump aboard and dutifully hand him his various buckets, rakes, burlap bags, plastic boxes, and two gasoline cans.

Soon enough, we back away from the dock, and I huddle behind the windshield of a cabin so small it holds nothing more than a steering wheel, compass, and radar box. Hillary deftly weaves the boat around the others that crowd the harbor, and then he aims for the two red cans that indicate deep channel waters. Venturing out toward open vistas, where much is downright unfamiliar, always acts as a panacea for me. Only Robin knows where I am, and even then, my destination is hardly precise.

"Is this just another workday for you?" I ask, noticing that Hillary's face exudes the same sense of anticipation and contentment that I feel. "Or is it about getting away?"

"Getting away," he murmurs, his voice muffled as he puffs on a cigar. "I've been shell fishing for thirty years—I like being out here by myself. Besides, every trip is a beautiful ride. Makes me feel happy to be alive. I don't know how long I'll be able to keep doing this. My new engine is probably going to outlast me," he says, chuckling at his sardonic humor.

Once we've cleared the channel, I feel very much the runaway woman—once again—someone who has just gotten rid of weekend guests and finally has the day to herself.

He shifts into full throttle and we're flying, the bow rising out of the water as we bounce across the surface, pushing through a confluence of currents to the open sea. Just then my water bottle rolls off the makeshift dashboard and toward the stern.

"Don't chase it," Hillary cautions above the roar of the engine. "Just hold on and take care of yourself." What a novel idea. Certainly if I let go now I would fall backward into his 115-horsepower engine or, worse still, be tossed overboard. So happily, despite myself, I take his suggestion.

"What takes you out here this time?" he hollers. "It's not every day I get a call in the dead of winter from a woman who wants to be dropped off on a barren beach."

"It's my anniversary," I say, as I pull my woolen hat down over my ears.

"Where's the husband?" he asks.

"Not that kind of anniversary. It's been ten years since I moved to the Cape. I thought I ought to venture out to the first beach I visited. I'm one of those crazies who likes to ritualize things. Besides, I'm curious about the new land bridge—kind of fascinating reading about the sand choking off the inlet."

We are zigzagging now, careening in great half circles, winding our way in and around numerous newly formed shoals and bars.

"No straight way out," I comment.

"Nope. Every ride is a little bit different from the last one. Keeps things interesting, especially at ebb tide, when the sea level is changing."

My mind perks up at the mention of ebb tide. Isn't that where I am in life right now—neither here nor there, but once again at a crossroads? "How would you define the ebb?" I ask him.

"It's the pause—the middle of things—no visible movement in any direction. The ebb is the moment when fresh seawater flows in or brackish water is flushed out—a kind of cleansing time."

Ebb and flow . . . ebb and flow. I take a whiff of the full salt moist air and then gaze aft to watch the wake being generated by the engine, just before Hillary shifts into low gear. "I'll need to be picking you up on the other side of Monomoy," he says. "The sea is dropping fast. Hope that's all right with you?"

"No problem," I answer bravely, although suddenly anxious. These waters and this shoreline are unrecognizable since I was last here.

"Are you familiar with Monomoy?" he asks.

"I've been out here before, but not recently. Each trip I planned got canceled for one reason or another. But I can't see that it will be too difficult for me to walk from east to west, especially if I use the lighthouse back in Chatham to maintain my bearings," I say, trying to sound confident.

"No matter. I'm good at spotting pretty ladies walking along any shore. I'll find you," he answers with a glint in his eye.

We are approaching several unexpected sandbars rising out of the emerald-blue water. "The recent full moon makes the highs and lows more extreme," he explains, holding on to the steering wheel with one hand while leaning over the side to make sure the water is deep enough for us to get through. "It's going to low faster than I anticipated," he mumbles, raising his engine out of the water to keep it from dragging along the bottom. "I don't clam much in this area. Can you make out any landmarks?"

Oh my, I hope he's not counting on me for direction. If I manage to get out here ten times a year, I'm lucky. Still, I feel a subtle pressure to carry my weight and so I furiously scan the distant beach for something recognizable.

With the engines cut, there is only the sound of waves slapping against the hull and the occasional barking gull. Adrift in the murky waters of the unknown, I suddenly want to reverse today's plan—return to port and enjoy the remainder of the day beside a warm fire. Just then, Hillary points east. "Wow, look at that washover," he exclaims, as I squint to see the high rollers toppling over the flattened beach and pushing into our calm bay. "That's one hell of a break," Hillary exclaims. "Seems when one inlet closes another opens up." He drops the engine and kicks on the motor so that we can continue to cruise toward our destination. I can sense him plotting our next move, trying to figure out what to do with me or, more to the point, how to get rid of me!

"Listen, when we get near the land bridge, wherever the hell it is—I'll need you to hop out fast or I'm afraid we'll run aground."

"Aye, aye, sir," I joke, taking that as a cue to roll up my sweatpants, slide my arms into my backpack, and zip up my waterproof parka. Hillary continues to scan the horizon.

"Oh my God," he shouts moments later as we both stare straight ahead at a white line of sand that evenly divides the sky from the sea. "There's the land bridge all right. I wouldn't believe it if I hadn't seen it with my own eyes—the inlet, closed up and gone forever. Boy, that's sure going to change a few people's lives. Everybody will have to adjust— fishermen, wildlife, even the tourists."

"You make it all seem so final," I say. "I must admit, I dislike change."

"No reversing this," he says, puffing on his cigar. "Nothing you can do about certain things. Besides, it might make things better. They talked about dredging, but it wouldn't have made a dent. When Monomoy broke in half a while back, everyone was doom and gloom because our scallop crop got buried, but guess what? We got steamers in their place, and they pay a lot better than scallops. You have to go with the flow. Natural accretion, it's called. This beach has rearranged itself. Now it's up to us to work with it. As for you and me, it's just about time to go our separate ways," Hillary says suddenly. "I've gotten as close to shore as I dare. So, woman, over you go."

I climb down the ladder fixed to the stern, attempting a delicate exit, but as soon as water hits my bare calves, the chill takes my breath away.

"Shit," I gasp, and then I'm out of the boat and pushing toward shore, a mere twenty paces away. I'm chilled and my toes have turned into icicles. My goal is to haul my body onto the embankment, don some dry socks, and put on my sneakers. What was I thinking, coming out here in the dead of winter, anyway? Hillary has already reversed the engine and is turning about.

Once on shore I stupidly look around for shelter, only to realize that there is none. I'm in bed with the elements for the time being. Hastily, I lace up my sneakers and then get back up to plot my journey. The expanse of beach before me is disorienting at best—a vast wasteland that looks as if it were recently bombed. The sand is covered with broken shells, fish bones, hundreds of horseshoe crabs, a seal carcass, and several dead gulls. With the pelting wind blowing sand in my eyes and every other uncovered orifice, it is hard to get my bearings.

I scan the horizon, looking for the dunes that dotted the landscape some twelve months ago. There appears to be a clump of something in the far distance and I slog onward. Fortunately the frozen sand allows for a brisk pace. I rush on, tiptoeing around the tufts of shimmering silver beach grass blowing in unison like clothes on a line hung out to dry. As I get closer, I discern the outline of a rough-hewn sculpture—huge pieces of driftwood, old planks from wrecked vessels, and large tree branches balanced against one another—created by a tourist most likely, and left to take on a life of its own.

The structure is designed like a tepee with multiple arms extending in every direction upon which a variety of refuse has been hung. In any other circumstance I would probably look for meaning in this edifice, but right now I'm too damn wet and cold. Fortunately, the architect of this rugged edifice has actually created a doorway, which in these chilly circumstances looks inviting, and I hastily duck inside. Although not totally airtight, it is better than sitting out in the open.

Grabbing a torn and greasy towel that is blowing from one limb, I stuff it into one of the larger openings to block the draft coming from the east, pull my hat down over my forehead again, double-wrap my woolen scarf, take out my thermos, and pour a cup of warm coffee, letting the smell and rising steam offer its early-morning greeting. Ah, the pure bliss of creature comforts!

It is only nine o'clock, and I have eight hours of wandering and musing before this adventure is over. Might as well take the time to enjoy breakfast. I lean back against a mangled lobster pot and gaze at the variety of stuff dangling from my fortress's limbs—a torn kite, several empty bottles and cans, a fisherman's rubber glove, tangled rope, a broken crab net, a chipped buoy, dried seaweed, and a yellow plastic "Live Strong" bracelet. It occurs to me that much of this trash is simply finished, left behind by one-time owners convinced it was useless. What good is a glove without two, or a bucket without a handle, a tackle box without a lid?

I remember moving out of our home back in New York and feeling rather melancholy—after all, it was the house in which we had raised our kids and developed our adult lives. Just before we left, a friend stopped by to say farewell and happened to make a comment that cut right to the core of my conflict. "Well, I suppose this house has outlived its usefulness, hasn't it?" he said. He was right. The boys had moved out years ago and left us with empty, unnecessary bedrooms; the big dining room never felt close and warm when Robin and I ate alone; and the yard, with an old tree fort falling apart in the back, and the garden, neglected once I got busy working, were more than either of us wanted to handle. I had a lifetime full of good memories attached to the house, but it was time for us to move on and start a new life in another home.

Now, as part of my ten-year inventory, I reflect on what is outlived in my life today. I've known for some time that holding on to anything ruins it, as does clinging to old ways, outdated ideals, worn-out relationships, and lifestyles that have run their course. As a culture, we seem to prize permanency. Certainly the familiar is comforting. But the way we were is not the way we are, and why would I want to still have those parts of my life that have lost their zest? Perhaps one of the reasons I felt so compelled to come out here today was actually to witness massive change. None of us can control the way life passes; we can only adapt.

Feeling warmed by a few embers of courage that seem to be coming from my thoughts, I take one last swig of coffee, slap my pack on my back, and crawl out of my shelter, anxious to walk along "the shore of the resounding sea," as Thoreau said, "determined to get it into me." I keep reminding myself of this old, faithful line. By merely setting out, there is always something bigger, better, and more life-giving to be found. This journey is not just about progressing through the world but about moving through stages of understanding.

I am pulled toward the ocean side by the incessant songful mourn of the winter sea, and soon I come across a lone dory, half sunken in the sand. Once a vibrant royal blue, its paint is now faded, chipped, and cracked; its hull half full of rainwater; one of its seats broken in two. This vessel is no longer seaworthy—it's a boat whose time is finished. I imagine that it sprang a leak time and again, and the owner simply caulked up each hole, until finally it was unsalvageable.

I can't help but compare this little dory to my mother, who is worn and tired, no longer able to be the vibrant vessel she once was. And like the dory owner, I am faced with the fact that there are very few repairs left that will make a difference. "It's up to Grandma now," our younger son, Luke, said after visiting her in the hospital during one of her illnesses. He knew her prognosis was not terminal, but he could see that she was weary. There was no one who could make her well but herself. She either wanted to live or did not.

As I further muse, I feel as though both my mother and I are swimming in the same sea—she's holding on to me, but I'm running out of energy to keep us both afloat. I have the strength to swim to safety on my own, but she does not. If I go under, we both do. So the choice is obvious, although enormously painful. I could never leave her alone as someone has left the dory, but I know I'm entitled to a life that does not always include her. Just as the owner of this boat came to recognize that he could no longer paint, caulk, and dig his boat out of the sand to make it seaworthy, so I realize that I cannot regenerate my mother's mind, will, determination, and agility. It's release from old age that she wants, and I can't give her that.

With resolution in my mind, but a heaviness in my heart, I move on toward the now infamous land bridge, stopping briefly to observe a colony of seals huddled on a sandbar quite far from shore—totally, contentedly safe from humans and boat traffic. They remind me of my boys, who seem perfectly happy with their distance from Cape Cod—one out west, the other in Illinois. My sense is that they relish their independence and their ability to reach out to Robin and me only when they please. In a cynical or sad mood, I would label them persnickety, just like the seals who tease and entrance but remain mightily independent.

Out here, when I can appreciate solitude and independence, I am able to say, "So be it." Would I want them attached like the barnacles to the old conch shell I just dropped in my tote bag? Would I want to have raised momma's boys who had no interest in flying the coop? No. I am proud of my boys and their thirst to forge original lives. But it hasn't been easy pushing them off as the mother seal does with her young days after birth, nudging them into the water to swim for their lives. When I urged them forward, I did not mean for them to settle halfway across the country. After all, forward could have been a heck of a lot closer!

One thing I know, a mother can never outgrow her love even for her grown children. Yet the intimacy she once shared, particularly with sons, over time becomes nothing more than simply "hope for loved strangers," as the Jungian Florida Scott-Maxwell once said. A good friend suggest that raising a child is the only relationship where, if you do it right, it ends in separation. She got that right!

Relatively speaking, we have only a small window of time for mothering. Although it seems when we are in this all-consuming phase as if it stretches on forever, in truth, such nurturing time lasts only ten to fifteen years. Then, poof, it's gone. Not unlike the first day of school for a child. It remains a vibrant memory, but in truth it was just a fleeting moment. So many of the big events in life are like that—monumental yet brief. Once again, recognizing that which is outlived is the answer. Remembering that helps me to accept the constant reconfiguration of family just as I am observing the reconfiguration of the beach before me. It is my issue, not theirs. Time to cross over to the other side.

8

Bridging the Gap

January

The best way out is through.

—Robert Frost

With a newfound sense of an inner heroine, I dare to walk, once more, toward my own salvation. With my trusty walking stick in hand, I hug the ocean's edge and keep my eyes on the sleek white strip of hardened sand ahead of me, fascinated by what nature has created, excited to be crossing over to what used to be unreachable on foot. Waves are encroaching onto the shore, their foam creeping up over the ridge of the bridge. Although the sky has turned dark and the day appears ominous, I've no choice but to proceed across the narrow spit of white sand that divides one body of water from the other.

As I approach the bridge, I encounter an odd sight—two sets of freshly made footprints on the hardened sand. Who could possibly be out here on such a foul day? On closer inspection, one set is clearly larger and belongs to someone with a lengthy gait, while the other was made by a small foot, taking two steps for every one of the other. It is easy to imagine that they belong to a man and a woman out for a walk together. I follow in their footsteps for a time, enjoying the feeling that I have some company, but then abruptly, the smaller footprints veer off toward the dunes, while the larger ones continue on over the bridge.

With little else to occupy my mind I become momentarily fascinated by this fictional couple who, for some reason, didn't choose to stay together in these deserted circumstances. Did they have an argument? Or are they simply a middle-aged couple, no longer in need of walking lockstep or being bound at the hip—not unlike Robin and me—in different places with different objectives? Most interesting, why am I upset that their footprints have separated?

It's a question I've been wrestling with a lot during these first years of Robin's retirement. With the kids raised and our careers in completely different phases, our directions vary, as does the speed with which we travel. Robin reads the paper, plays a round of golf, fusses over our finances, and works around the property. By six o'clock, he's ready for a drink. I, by contrast, wake up before the sun rises to log some quiet hours of writing, hurry out for a quick walk, and then run errands, check on my mother, and spend the latter part of the day returning phone calls. By six o'clock, I am ready for a shower, a sandwich, and bed. There are many evenings that we do make it to the beach, and many afternoons that Robin comes with me as I race around town. But the moments when we feel as if we are working together, toward a shared goal, are rare. In and of itself, the fact that we are moving to different rhythms doesn't create a lot of tension. But the difference between the way we are living and the way we thought we'd live in retirement is vast.

A nun I met recently guessed exactly where I was in terms of torment over relationship. "I wanted to mention something I saw in your book," she said, "something only alluded to but very significant." She had my rapt attention. "It is the human condition of wanting two states—of wanting to be alone and wanting to be in relationship. That pull seems to be implicit throughout your writing."

She hit me right between the eyes with a dilemma I live with each day. It seems to me that all of this soul-searching I've been doing at my midlife juncture is about meeting and being honest with myself once and for all. Well, if I am honest about my relationship with Robin, for the most part, I've been hiding out within it.

I pretend as if we've long since reached a stage where we are each encouraging the independence of the other, but I'm beginning to see that I've been using my work to stay somewhat apart from him. I love my husband and our marriage, but when he retired and moved to Cape Cod, just one year after I'd run off on my own, I still needed to feel more secure about my individual life—my life apart from my role as Joan Anderson Wilkins, Robin's wife. Furthermore, I was petrified that retirement would mean I had to follow him to an over-fifty-five community in Florida or Arizona. So I delved into my work, in part, to protect myself. It was easy enough to do—after all, the work was there. Besides, I have always agreed with Kahlil Gibran, who in *The Prophet* wrote: "Let there be spaces in your togetherness, and let the winds of the heavens dance between you. . . . Fill each other's cup but drink not from one cup. . . . Sing and dance together and be joyous, but let each one of you be alone."

Most long-term relationships, like the sea, ebb and flow;

they require time to be separate and time for reconnection. When the intensity of a relationship is allowed to rise and fall, romantic love turns into something more comfortable and heartwarming—a slow-growing devotion that includes both fierce and interesting companionship and a loyalty that provides support in an otherwise isolating world. But the ebbs aren't always as easy to handle as the flows.

Recently, I returned home after conducting a woman's weekend at which I had felt tremendously appreciated by the women who had attended. They were engaged and brought a great deal of energy to each workshop. By contrast, when I walked into the house, Robin barely took his eyes off the television to say hello, his mood utterly flat, lacking warmth or interest in where I had been.

Disappointed, downright hurt, yet too tired to start an argument, I simply headed upstairs to change my clothes. The bed was unmade, there were used towels on the bathroom floor, and a pile of dirty laundry waited to be washed. Why, I wondered, was he being so obviously thoughtless and uncaring? Perhaps it is simply because I have given *him* so little. If I put as much time and attention into my marriage as I do my work, I am sure I would reap similar rewards. Detail, thoughtfulness, presence—these are the ingredients that create the kind of intimacy we all crave. As Joan Erikson was known to say: "Relate is a verb. It takes action and thought in order to get a reaction." During the past few years, how much action and thought have I really put into my relationship? I fear I've taken comfort in the familiar, assumed the durability of my marriage was self-maintaining, and simply not reached for my husband as often as I could have. Entertaining such truth out here where I am helpless to remedy the situation increases my unease, further accentuated by the sighting of two black strips of clouds, the likes of which I've never seen before, as they are rising out of the sea and into the sky above.

I hesitate, for suddenly this adventure feels strangely menacing. Perhaps it's just the somber thunder of the surf—a sort of drumroll—the kind heard at a military funeral; perhaps it is that these insights into my own behavior are uncomfortable. Just then a flock of sea ducks fly in formation overhead and land on one of Monomoy's highest dunes, poised to greet me when I finally cross the bridge of sand. They seem to be urging me on, and so I lengthen my gait and push across this spit, born of wave and shaped by wind.

Then it happens. I step into a pool of mush. First my right leg drops, followed by my left—down, down, down I'm pulled, as if in quicksand, my torso suddenly buried, my backpack floating behind me. There I am, stuck like a capsized boat struggling to right itself. What's more, there is no escape—no inner tube to grab on to, no person to dive in after me. I will myself to be still while I come up with a plan to extricate my sinking body. Reaching for the little bit of solid shore I can see, I dig my fingers into the frozen sand and struggle to pull one leg free. The sand feels like wet cement, and my sneakers are acting like anchors. I am soon breathless and panicked. I try again as wave upon wave crashes upon me. I should have guessed when I saw the dark clouds that the day was beginning to turn, but I didn't expect this tidal wave of an experience. Then, by sheer will, I somehow loosen one leg and pull it free. Seconds later, I yank out the other and crawl as far away from the surf as possible, soaked but relieved.

If I had been determined to get the sea into me, I have certainly succeeded. What was meant to be a ritualistic walk to mark a new decade has become an exercise in survival. I clamber to my feet, readjust my backpack, and walk briskly to the other side, where the sea ducks are waiting, collapsing on the dune. As I process what has just occurred, and feel the relief that comes with getting oneself out of a jam, I think of all the weekend women I have brought out here.

There was the stutterer who embraced her infirmity and returned from her beach trek bold enough to sing about herself; the victim of anorexia who buried her scales and stopped measuring her worth by lack of weight; the thirty-eight-year-old widow and mother of three boys who released her grief in order to rejoin the human race; the mother of a dying daughter who came for respite so she could go back and continue the vigil at her daughter's bedside; and the third-stage-breast-cancer survivor who buried her survivor pin in order to be seen not just as one who has survived but as one who intends to live.

These and hundreds of other women have put themselves at the mercy of the elements to find the inspiration to redirect their lives. The women who visit this wild and salty place, where storms and seasons change the landscape from day to day, see with their own eyes the futility of holding on to old ways and illusions. Here they discover their own inner strengths, and realize that, in the end, there is no rescue after all. Each of us must and can save ourselves, just as I was given the chance to do a few moments ago.

As I smile at my little epiphany, grateful to be alive, I notice a man approaching dressed in fatigues, obviously military. He even has a gun in a holster.

"This is a restricted area," he announces, without preamble. The fact that he towers over me is unsettling.

"What?" I ask, startled, and quickly stand up.

"This area is off-limits to people. It's a nesting area for endangered birds," he says. "Didn't you see the signs?"

I don't bother to explain that I have just saved myself from oblivion and was only catching my breath. Somehow I know he won't care. So I walk over to read one of his signs:

NORTH AND SOUTH MONOMOY REGULATIONS
Portions of this area are closed to
ensure the success of nesting birds.

U.S. Fish and Wildlife Service

"Seems to me the operative word is *portions*," I say, realizing the importance of semantics at a time like this. "So which portion is available to human beings?"

The "bird man" doesn't seem impressed with my sarcasm. "Very little," he answers.

"Then we've got a problem," I say. "I'm supposed to be met by a fisherman on the other side of the island in an hour or two. That's my only way back to the mainland. Any suggestions as to how I might get there?"

"There's a cut about a mile down the beach, just before the lighthouse. If you don't deviate until you reach the path, I'll refrain from giving you the hundred-dollar fine for trespassing."

So much for feeling welcomed as one of the first to have come ashore on this remote island. I grab my things and quickly move on, not wanting to let this disagreeable man further ruin my day.

The fog is rolling in and I have yet to find the path. I step up my pace, reach a high ground beyond which I can spot the Sound, and cut west, albeit illegally, over the dunes, not wanting to miss my ride home.

Fifteen minutes later, I hear the deep thrum of a boat's motor and hope it is Hillary. Sure enough, emerging out of the mist is his faithful little boat with Hillary scanning the shore for that "pretty lady." Although I am relieved to be rescued, I am also triumphant about the walk I just took. I have made it to the other side, literally. The various storms have changed the shape of the island just as the challenges I have faced in the past ten years have changed me. But the good news is that I am the better for it. I untie my sneakers, toss them into my pack, roll up my pants, and splash headlong into the water, leaving the safety of shore behind.

Don't hold on to anything, I say to myself. There is more hope in a fresh future. A new season has begun, one in which I will let some fields lie fallow while others will be prepared for planting. As Joan Erikson was known to say: "All seeds have potential. It is time to stop stalling and start sowing."

9

On the Road Again

Late February

This above all, to thine own self be true,
And it must follow as the night the day,
Thou canst not then be false to any man.

—William Shakespeare

It is a cold February evening, a winter night when the snow is so light and fluffy that it blows about the road in such a way that I feel caught in one of those glass snow globes children get at Christmastime. I love this season—bound as I am in layers of woolens. It is a time to be tucked in, not only with clothes, but with dreams that have time to hibernate before emerging in the spring. Such are my thoughts as I head to the Salt Water Grill to celebrate my birthday with Ro and Susan. I felt a tinge of guilt as I set out, since I did not plan anything for either of their special days. But the remorse was fleeting. Even since my beach walk to Monomoy there's been an attitude shift. I am determined not to regress, and I've learned to recognize the red flags that start waving every time I so much as think about indulging in old habits. Much to everyone's surprise, I've managed to utter the word *no* almost as many times as the automatic *yes.* I have sent numerous personal and professional re-grets, and managed to get out of quite a few appearances and unrewarding obligations. I entertain my mother far less frequently, I'm not cooking every evening, and I'm letting some of the housework go.

The snow has been falling steadily for several hours

now, so I drive slowly. We considered canceling, but both Susan and Ro have blown off the last few dates we've made. For once I am not the only one with a packed schedule! Ro's been overextended ever since the premature arrival of her fourth grandchild, and Susan has been consumed with her new Greek lover. Every now and then I chuckle as I recall all their nagging to try to get me to pull back from my family entanglements.

I've just turned onto Monument Road and am passing the Church of the Holy Spirit—a special chapel I frequent from time to time because its simplicity offers solace and inspiration. When the old chapel needed to be rebuilt, each member of the congregation contributed something—a woodworker carved the pews, a glassworker crafted the stained-glass windows, someone else needlepointed the prayer cushions. Their collective effort seems to have imbued the space with more spirit than most churches I've attended. Lately, I find myself being pulled toward spirit, beginning to sense that the second half of life is meant to be more internal than external—a time for more feeling and less thinking. These recent thoughts have been affirmed by two Roman Catholic nuns who felt compelled to share their unsolicited sentiments on the subject with me.

The first, Sister Lita, feels as though she knows me intimately, having read all of my books. She has been e-mailing me recently, inspiring me to continue writing. "The theme of my Christmas letter this year was all about awe," she explained in her last note, "things that fill me with awe. When I wrote to you the first time I felt as if I were throwing a thought into space and maybe you would receive it. So I shook my head in wonder when you actually responded! As I look at all the skyscrapers here in Toronto, I think of the water going up all those stories and *then* coming back down . . . all invisibly . . . again I'm awestruck. As the saying goes, 'What is essential is invisible to the eye.' "

This last line stuck with me. I have spent so much time in nature getting messages about life by seeing and looking deeply into one unique or mysterious thing after another. But to know and, more importantly, to trust that which is invisible is another thing altogether. It is in this area I sense I still have work to do. I need to open myself up to the intangibles—qualities, sensations, intuitions that quicken the soul and make me truly feel alive.

The other nun sought me out to speak at a women's symposium. In the discussions leading up to the event, she shared what she sensed about my life. "It is obvious from your first book that you did a lot of soul-searching," she said thoughtfully, "but most of your conclusions seemed intellectually based. Then as you got to know and work with Joan Erikson's theories of actuality and went to Machu Picchu, your journey seemed more physical. But what you have yet to do, in my opinion, is to embark on a purely spiritual journey. Have you ever considered such a quest?" she asked.

"Of course I have," I assured her, "but it's been hard to find the time or place."

"Perhaps that is what's missing—what I sense you are craving and what your readers still need to hear." I couldn't have agreed with her more, but save visiting a local church or embracing the cloistered life, I remained hard-pressed to take her valued suggestion.

That is, until recently, when I received a letter from Mrs. MacDonald, a Scottish woman who, out of the blue, offered me her cottage on the isle of Iona. I came to learn that she is a philanthropist of sorts, who takes great pleasure in letting out her place to writers, artists, and seekers, particularly those active in the women's movement, ecology, and world peace. Evidently she stumbled upon my books in an airport and was moved enough to extend an invitation to me. I was perplexed, amused, and intrigued, but when I showed her letter to Robin, he promptly dismissed the invitation. "Didn't you intend to cut back on travel?" he said. "And where would the money come from for such a trip anyway?"

I reluctantly agreed, but I didn't toss the note away. Instead I tacked it to my bulletin board and continued to gaze at it whenever I needed a dream in my day. Each time I glanced at the invitation, I heard my Scottish father saying, "Sometime in your life, Joan, you must go to Iona." Certainly I could have received an invitation to visit any number of places in Scotland, but the fact that I had been invited to the very place my father had insisted I go seemed *too* coincidental. Secretly I hoped I would receive some further sign that this opportunity should not pass me by—after all, I had thousands of airline miles to take care of the cost of getting there and at least one nun pushing me onto more spiritual plains. The only real hurdle was leaving my mother, who, although now managing in her house with help, was nonetheless living the life of a recluse. But then, that excuse evaporated, as well!

Quite unexpectedly, she received an invitation to a cocktail party at the only assisted living facility she would ever consider. Never one to turn down free food and drink, she took herself off to what turned out to be an impressive affair. She returned home absolutely giddy, and I, for the first time, felt some hope about her situation. The very next day the administrator of the facility called to tell me that the best room in the place was available and that my mother could try it out for a month. This seemed just the final sign I needed.

So a few hours ago, after presenting my plans to Robin and e-mailing Mrs. MacDonald that I would love to use her cottage, I felt a surge of power, having given myself the best birthday gift ever. Thus, it is with jubilation that I skid into the parking lot of the restaurant, snowstorm or not, ready to party. It takes only a quick glance around the dining room to spot my friends at a corner table, festooned with balloons that they've tied to every chair. "You guys," I say, rushing toward them and giving each a peck on the cheek. "You shouldn't have, but I'm glad you did!"

"We've ordered what we think is a very appropriate wine," Susan says, dying for me to read the label after she pours me a glass.

I put on my glasses and hold the bottle up to the light— " 'Divas Uncorked—For Sisters Who Sip,' " I say. "How very appropriate."

They both look tired, Ro a bit more than Susan.

"How's the baby doing?" I ask. The rings under her eyes belie sleepless nights.

"The baby is fine. It's Hannah, the two-year-old, who's proving to be more of a handful. She wants and needs so much attention. We're bringing her to the Cape for a week soon to give her parents a bit of a break."

"In the middle of winter?" Susan gasps. "What will you do with her? I had a hard enough time having Jazz in October, but at least we could still go to the beach."

I feel for my friends, but I keep my mouth shut. They have never before understood how draining the summers are when everyone seems to visit.

The waitress appears with a sizzling tray of artichoke hearts stuffed with Gorgonzola cheese.

"Wow! Yummy," I say, digging in and savoring the warm, cheesy flavor.

"We went ahead and ordered a sort of tapas meal," Ro says, "so we don't have to agonize over the menu."

"You guys think of everything," I say. "It is so nice to feel taken care of." I sit back to take a sip of my wine, just as the entertainer for the evening, a folksinger, asks for everyone's attention.

"There's a woman over there in the corner," he says, pointing to me, "to whom I dedicate this next tune—an old Beatles song from the *Sgt. Pepper* album."

"Thanks a lot," I whisper to Ro, with a hint of sarcasm in my voice, as he begins to sing the McCartney tune "When I'm Sixty-Four." "Now everyone will know my age whether I want them to or not." Still, it's hard not to sway to the melody while others are tapping their toes and mouthing the lyrics.

How did I get to sixty-four anyway? I wonder as my eyes fill with tears. I began seriously accounting for my five and a half decades on South Beach ten years ago, and the good news is that my life is still unfolding. What's more, there is time to continue to refine and improve. I move back into the moment, listening hard to the lyrics that speak of hoped-for futures, and then, in a flash, the song is over. I blow a kiss to Ro, who was responsible for this musical gesture.

"So, how does it feel, being sixty-four?" she asks.

"I'm amazed to be here, but I feel forty, not sixty. All I know is that I want to be more intentional from here on out. The past decade is too much of a blur. Although it was a whirlwind and some amazing things happened, it somehow was surreal. Know what I mean?"

They both nod, especially Susan. "Having never really been in love before, I am forever praying that I will relish each fleeting moment. It's too good to be true, know what I mean? Simi and I are so grateful for each moment, but we wish we could turn the clock back."

"Some second journey you're on," I say.

"Huh?" Susan asks. "What's that?"

"Reaching for life in the middle of the ride," I explain. "Second journeys are usually thrust on people. They can be tragic or wonderful. Yours is surely the latter."

"That's for sure," Ro interrupts as the waitress brings us our next course, a platter of littlenecks.

"But all the upkeep must be exhausting—you know, all

those extra manicures, pedicures, having your hair frosted in a chic Boston salon. God, I can hardly remember what it felt like to date," I say. "How about you, Ro? Remember any of that?"

She shakes her head.

"You know we're just jealous as hell," I say, letting Susan off the hook.

"How about opening some presents?" she suggests, trying her own hand at self-deflection. She hands me a box with shells dangling from the ribbon. "Since you're a Pisces, I couldn't resist." Inside is a large bottle of moisturizing body balm called Ebb Tide.

"Thank you, but I sort of feel as if the tide has started to turn and I'm on the move."

"Really," Ro says, sounding mildly suspicious, as she has heard this tune too many times.

"I've told you that you do look different," Susan says, "more relaxed and without the wrinkled brow."

"That's because I've made some decisions just for me."

"Such as?" Ro says, still waiting for something concrete to come out of my mouth.

"Getting rid of the clutter—people, activities, and responsibilities. I'm done with anything that I find myself involved in halfheartedly. If I'm not fully engaged and feeling good about it, then it goes."

"Not our friendship, I hope," Ro chides.

"Hell no, but I am pleased to report that I've resigned from the board I've been complaining about, and I've canceled all my retreats until further notice."

"You did not!" Susan says with genuine surprise. "You've been threatening to for years, but I never thought you actually would."

"Take a look at my website—the events page is blank, and so is the retreat section. In fact, I let my secretary go just yesterday."

They are dumbstruck.

"Because, you see, I'm off to Iona in a couple of weeks."

"Where?" they ask in unison.

"An island in the Hebrides—off the coast of Scotland."

"Why would you want to go there?" Susan asks, utterly baffled. "I mean, shouldn't you be going to a spa or some tropical island where you might be pampered?"

"I know it sounds strange, but I'm Scottish, remember, and my father insisted that, somehow, I get to Iona. I feel as if I've been called."

"You're not going airy-fairy on us, are you?" Susan jests, her eyes rolling. "Why this place and why now?"

I fill them in on my unsolicited invitation from Mrs. MacDonald and the correspondence with the nuns.

"I'm dying to go exploring again—haven't had an adventure in years. Plus, making a connection with my heritage seems right. I bought an amazing Celtic CD, and I have taken to listening to one song over and over again. It sort of explains my calling. 'Have you forgotten who you are? Have you traveled so far? No trace of ancient story, But the tragedy of stone that stands alone.'"

"Well, it is not necessarily my cup of tea," Ro says, "but I can understand the pull for you since I'm drawn to Italy.

The one trip I made there brought out a part of me I hadn't known existed. My hands talked like theirs—I could see in the eyes of strangers my aunts and uncles. I'd still like to know the language better, know more of what makes them tick—get my great-grandmothers into my bloodstream somehow."

"So that's what you mean by a calling?" Susan asks.

"I see it as a yearning to go deeper," I explain. "The familiar everyday messages aren't cutting it anymore. I think many of us need to go in search of our history. It's the stuff of the classics—a hero going on a quest to become empowered from within. Ulysses stood on the shores of Ithaca and picked up the sweet smell of home, but only after a harrowing voyage away from Troy. At sixty-four my life is just beginning, and I need to move, once again, away from the predictable."

"To thine own self be true," Ro says.

"The Anderson motto is 'Stand Sure.' I'm hoping Iona will ground me once and for all."

As we are brought one dish after the next, I think about how much I love these women. One minute we can be gossiping and irreverent, the next grousing about our circumstances, and then we go deep into some idea that leaves us with a piece to take away and chew on. Joint contemplation, as I call these sessions, never fails to bring to the surface a modicum of much needed reality. Because of our passion for life as well as our friendship, we continue to prick one another out of mediocrity.

"I think it's a wrap, at least for tonight," Susan says after the last dish is cleared away.

"Happy birthday, dear friend," Ro says.

We head out into the blustery cold, fortified by the warmth of friendship. As I creep home, the windshield wipers barely keep up with the huge snowflakes. There are the outlived events and relationships that we must celebrate and then let go of, and there are the unlived experiences that we must search for, welcome, and live into. I may not be able to see the road, but my immediate future is clear.

10

Traveling Ancient Highways

Late March

*We are not human beings making a spiritual journey . . .
we are spiritual beings making a human journey.*

—*Pierre Teilhard de Chardin*

The whistle of the ferry startles me, and then I feel a surge of pure excitement as the heavy boat backs away from the dock and the seaside town of Oban becomes a fleck in the distance. I stand at the railing and breathe deeply, hoping to inhale some of the magpie magic that permeates the islands to which we are headed. A light swell soothes any anxiety I might have brought aboard, and, for a time, I am content simply to gaze at the scenery—a tall white lighthouse guarding the large harbor, a wonderful medieval moss-covered castle, a pod of seals dancing in the ferry's wake. I am crossing to safety, or so it feels, heading for Iona to become a virtual vagabond, doing as Robert Frost suggested and taking the road less traveled.

Hardly anyone goes to Iona, I'm pleased to say, because it's too damn hard to get there. My journey of three thousand miles began some thirty-six hours ago. I had an overnight flight to London, then a shorter one to Glasgow, after which I took a three-hour train trip into the highlands, spent the night in Oban, and boarded the ferry this afternoon. Now I am finally beginning to feel as though the real journey has commenced. The hardest part is behind me—breaking away, making the decision to come on such a venture in the first place, and convincing myself that I wasn't being self-indulgent. This is what the women who come to my weekends must feel like.

Many of them travel so very far and are both excited and anxious, wonderfully free and nervous about the unknown steps they are about to take. Compared with all of the preparation, this voyage to the island of Mull is too short—a mere hour and a half, hardly enough time to decompress, slow down, and switch from the frenzied pace of the mainland to the serenity of island life. I settle into a deck chair to let the ship rock me into otherworldliness, intending for this journey to be one that gets me out of my head and into my heart. I want the second half of my life to be every bit as meaningful as the first.

Joan Erikson first taught me the value of walking off the beaten path when in search of new direction and spiritual revivification. That is precisely what she did when she ran off to Europe to find Isadora Duncan. There was no such thing as modern dance in America at the time, but she knew that her body could express itself in more ways than those defined by classical ballet. And so, on a hunch, she sold most of her worldly belongings, bought a steamship ticket, and went in search of something that would speak to her soul.

"Learning from life is much more beneficial than learning from a book," she would say, "because you are taking action. Action always creates reaction as well as change." Joan's unconventionality cheers me on, as I am prepared to step over the threshold. And Iona, tucked away as it is at the edge of the world, is the perfect place for a pilgrimage. I feel as though I have been summoned to where I can find clarity and transformation.

As the engines grind and we plow through the choppy waters, a cup of coffee sounds good, and I head for the snack bar, where there is a substantial line. Already I can sense a change in my attitude. Lines at home, in the supermarket or post office or airport, usually tie me up in knots. But today, I am enjoying the conversations, the mannerisms, and the people around me. From the moment I set foot on Scottish soil, I felt as though I'd come home: my ruddy complexion, round face, lust for life, and willfulness are characteristic of the highlanders who surround me. Kilted Scotsmen were all over the airport, already a bit tipsy at ten in the morning, scurrying off to a soccer tournament with Ireland. The lone piper piping them off brought tears to my eyes because I could see my father in many of the men's faces. "Continuity with the past is not a duty," Oliver Wendell Holmes said, "it is only a necessity." Life is too difficult to survive without revering one's ancestors, honoring and attempting to know those who came before me even as I try to upgrade the gene.

I order my coffee and a scone, and then move back to an inside seat near a window so I won't miss a moment of the passing sea. It is fun to be in a place where no one expects any-thing of you. Quite simply, I have no need to impress the peo-ple I see here, and that, in and of itself, allows me to relax. In this foreign land, I can set aside all of the demands of others. I have no one here to accommodate—no obligations to meet ex-cept ferry and bus schedules. I have come halfway around the world to be unattached, and it feels divine. No more pushing against the current. Instead I'm going with the flow.

I gaze around at my fellow travelers and wonder about their reasons for being on this boat. The bevy of children gathered around the snack bar surely must be bound for

Tobermory—recently put on the map because of a BBC children's series by a similar name. There is a pretty, young, self-conscious girl, probably a student, another attractive twentysomething woman looking admiringly at her lover, several tired-looking pregnant women, and a mother with twin boys in a stroller. I can't help but feel relieved that those phases of my life are behind me—fulfilling as they were, it is time to be someone for myself. It is exhausting to realize just how much I have experienced and how much of that past life defines who I am now. I lean my head back as the ferry cuts through the deep green sea.

Just then a young Dutch woman approaches and startles me by saying, "You must be going to Iona."

"I am. How did you guess?" I ask.

"The sticker on your bag," she says, pointing toward my backpack and the phrase "Unfinished Woman." "Iona is the destination for many of us in search of the goddess. It's a very feminine island, you know."

The idea of Iona being feminine is intriguing and adds another layer of meaning to why I've been called. Lately my masculine side has all but overtaken me—driving, pushing, doing, accomplishing. I think what I have been craving is balance—a return to being more quiet, internal, soft, simple, welcoming, and receiving. As May Sarton said,

Now I become myself. It's taken
Time, many years and places;
I have been dissolved and shaken,
Worn other people's faces,

Run madly, as if Time were there,
Terribly old, crying a warning . . .

A self-imposed pilgrimage is a quest, Joseph Campbell suggested, where you might not know what you're looking for but you have acknowledged that you're looking for something. "If you are ready then the doors will open where there were no doors and there will come aids as well as difficult trials." For certain, nothing that occurs is incidental.

Campbell also insisted that the pilgrim had to give up something to get something, so before leaving home, I obeyed the rules for a successful pilgrimage by giving up the projects that were weighing me down. I let go of my children, released my mother to assisted living, and trusted that my husband would understand my quest. Everyone kept pestering me about the pace of my life, my frenzied schedule, and my racing blood pressure. But I knew that was only one part of the problem. The other part was still unknown. I was uncomfortable going forward in my life without going deeper. Like walking around with a pebble in your shoe, I was constantly reminded that I hadn't yet arrived at that place of peace, where I possessed a natural energy that emanates from within, not energy that is derived from sheer effort and will.

It was one thing to know my strengths—those Eriksonian virtues such as Hope, Will, Purpose, Competence, Fidelity, and Love that grow through resolving conflicts. But I was aching for those qualities not obtained from struggle, those intangibles such as pure joy, passion, vulnerability, inner contentment, peace of mind. I did not have nearly enough soul-filled moments in my daily life, and I knew I would remain stuck in the vast wasteland of my topside world if I didn't take action.

In short, I sensed that there was more to get at, that as Henry Miller suggested, "Every person has his own destiny . . . the only imperative is to follow it, accept it, no matter where it leads."

Recently a forty-four-year-old man approached me after a talk I gave in which I spoke about the difference between significance and success, and said that purpose is more important than power. He was president of his own company and seemingly had everything, yet his mother had died three weeks earlier and her death had left him empty. Suddenly he was seeking much more than success and power. "How could I have that?" he asked, wiping tears from his eyes.

Inner knowing, I wanted to say, but that would hardly explain anything. How does one reverse the constant pushing through life to capture success and refocus one's attention on having an active internal life? Unfortunately, there is no straight course that will lead any of us to the intuitive, instinctive, and spiritual place inside us. I didn't have an answer for this man, because I myself was just starting to turn my own attention inward.

So I simply quoted Carl Jung: " 'For people over thirty, all problems are spiritual rather than psychological,' " I said. " 'Although you are overly involved in external goals, you will only be able to come to terms with what really matters if you pause, break from the mundane, and process the grief that is partner to change.' "

And that is precisely what I am about to do. The ferry whistle has just sounded, announcing our imminent arrival in the town of Craignure on the island of Mull. I race toward the bow, wanting to spot the pencil line of shore as soon as it emerges out of the mist. There appear to be a few small houses and a rather large dock. The only other sights coming into focus are the deep Cabernet-colored moors and mountains.

Feeling as though I've already crossed over to Avalon, I grab my suitcase, head for the gangway, and follow the other passengers onto the dock. A quick glance over my shoulder at the busyness that I've left behind is all I need to say farewell—out loud actually—to cell phones, e-mail, newspapers, media, and especially people, most of whom are well meaning, but hardly any of whom are on this very strange path I have chosen.

I head for the buses, all of which are lined up to take us to one of two destinations. The doors are wide open for Tobermory, but the one bus intended for Fionnphort and the ferry to Iona is locked, with no driver in sight.

"We won't be going there 'till later in the day," a ticket agent informs me. How am I going to occupy myself for several hours in such an obviously inactive village? I decide to seek the advice of a friendly-looking lady working a concession stand a few feet away.

"Aye, you're headed for Iona?" she asks, her brogue so thick I can barely make out a word.

I nod my head in the affirmative.

"Sorry, mate. Since hardly anyone goes to Iona this time of year, they only run one, maybe two buses a day. And why would you be going there, if you don't mind me asking?" Her curiosity is more than piqued.

"To write," I say. "I'm an author."

"You don't say," she continues, her daily entertainment obviously coming from tourists like me who stop by her stand for postcards, maps, and local foods. "You'll find some magic on Iona," she says.

Although I wasn't necessarily looking for magic, I suppose deep down I was hoping for some signs that I was moving in the right direction. "So can you give me a suggestion—is there any other way I can get to Fionnphort?"

"I'll call Iain McGinnis, if you like. He runs a taxi service. Might cost you more than a ha'penny," she jokes. "I'll just run off to my house and ring him up. Would you mind the store?"

I walk to the other side of her little shack and stand waiting for a customer, all the while gazing out at the ferry, now about to return in the direction from whence it came. As it pulls away from the dock, I feel that peace—or is it freedom?—that I am alone and no one can interrupt my thoughts or deeds. A good beginning to a pilgrimage, I think.

"He'll be right along," my new friend announces a few minutes later, feeling smug that she could so easily solve my problem. "Have yourself a meat pie—my treat."

I choose minced pork and onion tucked inside some very good crust and devour it until moments later when a tiny yellow Citroën pulls up, and out steps Iain McGinnis—a red-haired, strapping young man dressed in woolen knickers and a very worn-looking tweed jacket. He tips his shabby hat, shakes my hand, and promptly loads my luggage in the trunk. With no time to offer a proper good-bye to my lady friend, we're off, driving faster that I had ever envisioned possible on a one-lane road with traffic coming from the other direction.

"Heading for Iona?" he asks. "Will you be working at the abbey?"

"No, just going there, I suppose, to unwind."

"You've picked a good place," he says. "Nothing there but fifty or so houses, one hotel, and a very busy pub—not much to do but work hard and then have a dram or two at the end of the day."

"Really," I say, momentarily wondering how I will spend three weeks in such isolation.

"They call it I'shona—that's Gaelic for blessed or spiritual isle."

"Well, that's good news. I'm looking for something spiritual—just not sure what."

"Aye. You best head over to the west for the rocks—the beach is loaded with them. You only need touch them and you'll feel something. They say it's earth energy, some sort of magnetic force." His quiet conviction is haunting.

"Well, the lady back in Craignure told me that there was magic on Iona. Maybe that's what she meant?"

"There are strong energy spots," he explains. "I've hiked the island. If you're looking for answers, you'll find them in the moors. Not just in the rocks, but in the air. I think the Druids left their wisdom behind—whispered directions, they say."

"You know so much," I suggest.

"Born and bred here. Don't bother with the mainland much."

I find his contentment strange for someone so young since so far I've seen only a couple of B and Bs, sheep grazing everywhere, and that's about it. We pull over to let a bus pass by, and when we start up again, I ask him the time.

"Eleven forty-five. Good chance we'll make the ferry, if that's what you're wondering." He steps on the gas pedal and speeds up a bit, braking now and again for cattle to cross or a mother sheep to nudge her babies off the road. We are soon winding around a huge bend that has a view of a tiny harbor, and then I spot the ferry, cars already driving aboard, walk-ons not far behind. We screech to a stop right next to the gangway, and after pressing thirty pounds into his hand, I run off, the last passenger aboard.

"Lucky you made it, lady," the ferryman informs me. "This is the last trip of the day. As it is, we expect a rough crossing. You best take a seat."

I tuck inside the nearest cabin as the small but sturdy boat begins to pitch and roll immediately. Against his instructions and fearful of getting sick, I head for the deck and some air as the little ferry plunges and bucks against the strong currents. Waves are crashing over the hull as I grab hold of the rail to steady myself. The trip, meant to take fifteen minutes, will take double that in these stormy seas. We must head up against the tide in order to drift back toward the dock.

The salt spray has me drenched, but never mind—my anticipation of this moment overtakes being wet and uncomfortable. And then I hear an announcement: "This ferry will be able to withstand the currents at dock for no more than two minutes. You are advised to gather your belongings, proceed to the lower deck, and be ready to disembark immediately. Take care with your footing as the dock itself might be quite slick."

I head for the stairwell, which is no more than a ladder, and back down, ready to jump ship. The engines are soon grinding as the captain shifts the boat into neutral, and then I watch as the gangway is lowered into a crashing sea. I run, plowing through knee-deep seawater, my suitcase, leggings, and hiking boots now all soaked through, but no matter—I'm on Iona. As the ferry departs, instead of feeling disoriented and abandoned, I feel strangely at home, even though there is no one to greet me. I head for the island's only hotel, an unpretentious three-star establishment a mere five hundred paces down a narrow cobblestone street. Just inside the door of the Argyll is a coatrack filled with slickers, a container with umbrellas and walking sticks, and nearby, on a table that holds a guest book and some pamphlets, sits a beautifully hand-carved seal. He is beaming right up at me— the very creature that has taught me so much—the one that gave me clues at the beginning of my journey ten years ago.

I leave my backpack and suitcase in the hall and wander toward the reception desk, where there is a bell to ring for assistance. Taped to the counter nearby are instructions: "Ring Vigorously"—the very same words Joan Erikson had attached to a bell for her visitors to ring. I am stunned by the serendipity of first the seal and then this. In a few minutes,

Daniel, the proprietor, appears. "Didn't expect anyone off the ferry today," he says. "You prepared to stay on for a few months?" he quips. "You could be stranded forever."

"Actually, I have a house to use just down the street, I believe. A Mrs. MacDonald left a key with you."

"Oh, you must be the American," he says.

"I am that," I answer. "Is your hotel open to outsiders for dinner?"

"Indeed," he said, putting my name in the reservations book for a week's worth of dinners. "Would you like a spot of tea until this awful rain lets up?" he asks.

"That would be lovely," I say and head toward a chair near a fire made of peat and coal. I had an agenda all lined up, intending to begin immediately at the abbey and then hike north to a beach known for its healing effects. But the weather won't allow that, so I settle into a chair and watch as the hotel staff bustle around serving six or seven guests their late lunch.

My tea arrives momentarily, and I am once again stunned. The brown and black pot is precisely the same pottery my paternal grandmother owned. She must have brought it from the old country. Although the expression "there are no coincidences" is grossly overused, I cannot help but feel that I was truly meant to be in this place, here and now. There have been too many signs that I could no longer ignore. "Go where your best prayers take you," said the theologian Frederick Buechner, and as I pour my tea and add several lumps of sugar, I know I have.

11

Abbey Road

Early April

*I have discovered, you do not need to know what
you are looking for—only that you are looking
for something, and need urgently to find it.
It is the urgency that does the work, a readiness
to receive that finds the answers.*

—Janine Pommy Vega

Sleet and snow beat against the window in my little cottage. The wind is so fierce that it awakens me, and I peer out. The daffodils that brightened the island yesterday are now bent over, heavy with frost. Spring is such an intermediary season—rarely is it this or that, just like me right now, as I sense that I'm back in the ebb, ready to grow and expand, and yet stopped by an unexpected and strange inertia.

If, indeed, I have metaphorically crossed over to Avalon, then that accounts for the fact that I have felt drugged ever since I arrived some four days ago—almost in a trance— feeling that I have awakened from a deep sleep only to ask, Where am I? How did I get here? What am I supposed to do now? It's the last question that has me troubled the most. It was one thing to take a leap, pack my bags, board a flight, and for the most part, not know or care where I might land. During that part of the adventure, I felt as if someone else was in charge. But now that I am here, it is solely up to me to make my days count. I intended for this to be a pilgrimage of sorts, but I haven't the faintest idea what that actually entails, save wandering about and being open to the whim of this place and its people.

Here on this island with no mountains to scale, no destinations to reach, no straight paths to follow, I remain puzzled. Still I harbor hope that the supposed potent energy of Iona will propel me straight to the heart of the matter. I traveled a long way to change my life, and this loopy state I am in right now has left me frustrated. But I remind myself that no matter where I am, pounding away for a thought or answer isn't the way, nor is pleading or cajoling the angels. Besides, I'm happily ensconced in a whitewashed crofter's cottage.

At first I felt like an intruder—bloody lonely, actually, living solo in this space without any official greeting. My initial reaction was to rush back to the security of the Argyll. But no sooner had I opened the curtains and put on the teakettle than I found all sorts of greetings from a hostess who, I'm told, is rarely on the island during the off-season.

The cottage is sparsely furnished with castaways apparently from her other house somewhere on the mainland. It is a cozy place complete with parlor and kitchen in one room, two small bedrooms, and a tiny bath with an old-fashioned tub on legs. The walls are paneled and painted a mustard yellow, and there is a white enamel kitchen table circa 1935, upon which my hostess left a bottle of port, several kinds of tea, and a half bottle of single-malt Scotch. Plenty of kindling, coal, and wood are piled near the fireplace. But I felt truly at home when I spotted a blanket draped over the armchair by the fireplace—a woolen comforter made from none other than the Anderson tartan.

Although Mrs. MacDonald and I had never spoken about the fact that I would be writing while in residence, an old pine writing table was placed in front of a round window resembling a porthole on a ship. She had filled an old tin can with freshly sharpened pencils, left several legal pads on the desk, one ink pen complete with inkwell, and numerous works of Keats and Wordsworth placed nearby. I did feel I should produce at least a poem or short story while here. "Welcome, Joan," a note read. "It is my wish for you that Iona will provide just the muse you need to create whatever it is you were meant to do while on this mystical island. Fondly, Mary MacDonald."

Still, being in such a new and foreign place was momentarily invigorating, until I realized there was no one to actually show me the way. I hadn't expected a formal guidebook indicating points of interest and well-marked trails, but at the very least I was hoping for a suggestion or two in Mary MacDonald's personal note of welcome. The only bit of direction I could find was a Celtic wish hung on the wall near the door, and I quickly adopted it as my first set of instructions.

May the nourishment of the earth be yours,
may the clarity of light be yours,
may the fluency of the ocean be yours,
may the protection of the ancestors be yours.

Now that the initial state of euphoria has dissipated, I need to figure out how to get inside myself. They say Iona is a state of mind into which one gradually drifts, and I'm hoping that's the case. I'm more than aware that spiritual truths are hard to come by and enlightenment requires real time spent in solitude, but I have only two and a half weeks left. Besides, profound silence is not something I fall into easily, although I thoroughly believe wisdom would more readily befall me if only I could just keep my mouth shut. So often in conversations I interrupt the speaker. It is not because I don't like what he or she is saying, it's because I get carried away by the energy of the conversation itself. But I know that each time I jump in and add my thought right over someone else's I've utterly changed and probably diluted what the speaker was trying to say to me. So silence remains one of my great challenges.

According to the Buddhists, the goal of a pilgrimage is to exist totally in the present—a good idea, but another difficult one for someone who tends to daydream about the future because she wants immediate answers to questions. I sense that achieving such presence depends on idleness, another challenge, as I prefer motion. So here I sit, looking out the window as the ferry comes and goes, trying to journal my thoughts, which aren't coming, and when all else fails, frequenting the pub down the street—a public place—the only one in which I feel welcome.

Still I am resolved that this day must be different from the past three. Even though the sun cannot make up its mind whether to brighten the island or remain behind threatening clouds, I am determined to launch my quest in earnest.

I look for the clock, and then remember there isn't one—nor a radio or newspaper. That's another thing that's disconcerting to a mainlander whose life is geared to knowing the time, being on time, having enough time, and of course, the demon of all type A personalities, being sure to make the most of my time. All I know for certain is that the sun has risen, the first ferry has come and gone, and if I hurry, I am likely to make the eight o'clock service at the abbey. Out I go, into the fierce wind, scarf wrapped around my neck, woolen hat pulled down practically over my eyes, rushing up the main street just as I hear the great bell ringing.

"Seek and ye shall find," it says in the Bible, and seeking I am, trudging the mile or so to take sanctuary in the drafty stone church that offers a sense of history as well as peace. I huddle in the very back row, watching the candles flicker in the huge wrought-iron candleholders that dot the nave. The austere surroundings exude a sort of majesty—as if indeed a deity is hovering about in the rafters along with the wind and cooing doves. I take a deep breath, then another, knowing that the word *spirit* comes from the Latin *spirare*, meaning "to breathe."

Although being here takes my mind off worldly issues, I am not particularly moved by the service—conducted today by a stern-speaking Englishman. Still the sections of the Mass that are sung, not spoken, reach the remotest corner of my sensibilities and I immerse myself, for the first time, in the possibility of Iona. I feel finally in "sanctuary" and blessed that this abbey offers, if nothing else, a refuge—the beginning or at least the hope of something more transcendent to come.

The short service over, the parishioners seem in a hurry to get on with their day. I huddle in my chair, eyes closed, waiting for the place to clear out, wondering what the abbey might offer when it is not on display. I have stilled my mind and opened my heart, why not stay open to what happens next? While the church empties, I listen to the wind, even the sea, all the while staring at one lone flickering candle. The elements are working together, finding a common rhythm, and I am being pulled in—having my own service right now—my spirit engaged as I breathe in unison with the wind and sea. It dawns on me that I am being held by all four elements. The air filled with incense permeates, the rock walls lifted from the earth now encapsulate, water dripping over the baptismal font soothes, and the flames from candles offer warmth. My soul expands and I sink into a timeless state.

After a while, I begin to walk around and explore— approaching the altar, studying the cross made of Iona's famous green marble, amused that greenery is pushing through the stone and beginning to drip down, partially covering the walls on either side of the choir. And then I spot a small chapel, called the Quiet Corner. It is adjacent to the main church but very much hidden—perfect for those of us who seek retreat. In the dim light I find an elderly man in one corner, hunched over, his hands folded on top of his cane. Quickly I slip into the nearest chair and pretend not to notice him, gazing instead out of the two windows that face the sea and eventually closing my eyes.

Minutes later, he whispers: "You're the American, aren't you?"

I lift my head, stunned. Didn't know anyone had actually noticed my presence on this island.

"I am," I quietly admit. "I do hope you don't hold it against me?"

He smiles, the kindliest smile that has been bestowed on me since I arrived.

"Have you found what you're looking for?" he asks.

"What?" I say, taken aback. "I'm afraid I've come with too full of an agenda," I whisper, "trying to get too much out of your island in too short of a time."

"Just be still," he says, "wherever you are. Iona is no Utopia . . . there is no such thing. It's all here," he says, pointing to his heart. And with that piece of unasked-for wisdom, he walks over to the organ, removes its cover, opens its lid, and begins playing. I had wished for that sound—a great organ, filling this place—the acoustics certainly built for sung vespers and liturgical instruments. I lean my head back and listen as he plays Bach's Fugue in D minor without so much as looking at a sheet of music. He continues on with several Anglican hymns I barely recognize, and as I watch him play I can see how he is lost in the act of making music. I rise and stop beside the organ, waiting for him to finish something from Vivaldi so I can thank him.

"Pray, but don't expect anything," the old man cautions. "A few minutes with a painting, a sunrise, or even listening to a string quartet will give you more than what you need."

I wander out into the cold, the day now brightening a bit. With hours to go before I sleep and feeling overly stimulated, I decide to stop in the community bookstore, a place I've been tempted to visit in the hope that they might sell instruction for a novice on how to actually do a pilgrimage! But since I came here to stay out of my head and get more into my body, I've resisted until now the temptation to buy books that would create more thought.

Once inside I'm greeted by an American volunteer who comes to Iona to work every year. "So, another American amongst us," she says cheerily. "We've been talking about you. Seems you've written a book for women about finding themselves. So what are you searching for here?"

Again, I'm caught off-guard. How did such information find its way to this stranger? I am now aware that on an island that boasts not more than a hundred inhabitants, any news is news. Single women who appear in the rainy season are conspicuous. For sure they're on one mission or another.

"You know what it's like back home," I say to this stranger who already feels like a friend. "Actually, I'm on a vacation of sorts and Iona has always been on my wish list. I came to escape all the show, the noise, and the reactiveness of life at home. I was told I'd find more quiet and thoughtfulness here. So how did you find Iona?" I ask, enjoying the chance for some lively conversation with another woman.

"Came on a day trip with my husband years ago. On the ferry, crossing over from Mull, I met a man who was working here. He told me there were lots of jobs available if you didn't mind communal living. I was mildly intrigued until I stepped off the boat. It was like—wham! This was my place. Unfortunately, or fortunately, my husband didn't share my sentiments. But I couldn't fathom leaving. He went on, and I stayed the summer."

"And the marriage?"

"Oh, that's long gone. Iona helped with the split," she says, chuckling in delight at how her life has turned out. "You are looking for something, too—I can feel it," she pushes.

"Yes," I say. "But I can't really explain it."

"That's all right," she says. "I understand. But if you want a suggestion . . ."

"Sure would," I say.

"You must go to Dun-I. It's the highest point on the island—not that that means anything. But it's a sacred spot, designated so by the Druids. Going at sunrise and drinking from what is called the pool of healing will change your perspective on everything."

She notices my doubtful expression, walks to a bookshelf, reaches for a book written in 1910, turns to page 164, and reads from a rather dated description of what she is talking about. " 'To this small, black brown tarn, pilgrims of every generation, for hundreds of years have come so as to touch the healing water the moment the first sunray quickens it— but solitary also, because those who go in quest of the Fount of Youth are the dreamers and the Children of Dream and these are not many. Yet an isle of Dream Iona is, indeed.' "

"Sold," I say, buying both the book and her suggestion.

"But you must get up there before sunrise," she cautions.

I feel, at last, that I have received the direction I was hoping Iona would offer. "You can't find God (the spirit) apart from humanity," Gandhi said, and I'm finding that is so true here. I head off to the Argyll for a big Scottish breakfast and a good read.

12

Crossroads

April

The leap of faith is not so much a leap of thought as of action. One must . . . dare to act wholeheartedly without absolute certainty.

—William Sloane Coffin

It is 4:00 A.M. and the alarm has just awakened me. I borrowed a clock from the Argyll to make sure I wouldn't miss the sunrise, but the wind is howling so strongly outside my little window that I have my doubts about whether I'll be able to make out anything. On closer inspection, I see that it is covered with frost. Am I out of my mind? Just because a woman, and an American no less, makes a suggestion doesn't mean I need to listen. No matter, I wouldn't be able to go back to sleep now.

I reach for my silk underwear, top that off with a turtleneck and sweatpants, and just to be on the safe side, don my waterproof parka. There's no time for a cup of coffee. Dawn is predicted for 5:15, and I haven't the faintest idea how long this trek will take. I only know that it's straight uphill. Complete with muddy walking boots, a flashlight, and a walking stick, I head out, feeling altogether foolish as I quietly make my way down the now familiar quay toward the tiny street that leads out of town.

Nonetheless, there is something magical about walking through the darkness, gazing up at the galaxy of stars just beginning to fade into a morning sky. I move slowly, barely able to see in front of me, pushing aside the mist until I come to a hand-carved sign that has an arrow pointing to

Dun-I. I push open the gate and minutes later find myself in someone's soggy pasture where long-haired cattle stare up at me and sheep dash off, herding their lambs with them. Although I am fairly sure-footed, the springtime soil, coupled with the dull light of predawn, makes this venture more of a challenge than I would have expected. I spot a narrow opening in a craggy wall of stone, moss, and grass straight ahead and guess that the path will lead somewhere. Despite sheep poop and questionable terrain, I am mildly exhilarated to be trying something so utterly new.

It is indeed one straight shot up, just as the book said, and I start to breathe heavily. But the physical effort is countered by the softening I feel inside, as if I am thawing out and climbing right out of this world into another. The sky keeps getting lighter, and I am better able to sense how far I still have to climb. I have slipped twice and am covered in mud, but the summit is unmistakable as I spot a large cairn built by climbers over the years. Another twenty minutes or so and I approach this rock altar, some twenty feet high, built, no doubt, with reverence by all who have made this trek before me. I lean back against the wall it provides, face the glow that precedes the sun, and experience a stillness like I have never known before. Although I had a sense of sanctuary in the abbey yesterday, here, with a 360-degree view of this little island waking up, I realize that sanctuary is never just a building, no matter how revered, ancient, or holy. Rather, it is a state of mind—of being.

"There are these moments when the soul takes wings," wrote Fiona MacLeod, one of the first to describe Iona's spirit, sitting on this very spot some one hundred years ago. "What it has to remember, it remembers; what it loves, it loves still more; what it longs for, to that it flies."

I look down at the world beneath me—the first ferry about to make its crossing, white dots of sheep, some black and brown spots of cows, a walker on the way to work, a partially lit abbey preparing for breakfast—a little village waking up as it has for hundreds of years. Why is it so difficult for me to remember the need to simply sit periodically and watch time unfold?

The sky is truly blue now, save for the burnt orange peering up from behind the mountains of Mull. I've got little time to find my holy pool of water, and I begin wandering around the mound, looking down a crevice here or over a boulder there. Just as the sun peeks above the rim, I spot an unimpressive puddle half hidden under heather and quickly kneel beside it, cupping my hands to splash as much water on my face as I possibly can. With my face chilled and dripping, I open my eyes and look downward, expecting to see the reflection of a woman who is haggard and tired. Instead I hold very still so as to make certain that the tranquil expression and unforced smile looking back at me are truly mine. Something sets loose inside and I begin to cry—happy tears at first, and then the deeper tears I've held back for years because there never really was a convenient time to be emotional.

After a while, I start to feel silly—what am I doing on a mountaintop at dawn, performing an ancient purification ritual? I look around to make sure no one is watching me. Ro and Susan surely would laugh at my airy-fairy endeavors.

I pull back from the edge and lean against a nearby rock to set in my mind this place and this picture. It soon becomes apparent that this little pool is a triangle—a fact that would have made no difference to me if I didn't know the Celtic peoples have particular reverence for this shape. They see three as the perfect number. Standing up now, I survey the pool from various vantage points. I'm reminded of the triple Goddess—a Celtic idea of women whom they saw as developing from maiden to mother to crone, and that I have become such a woman, one who has passed through life's earlier stages and as such has much to offer. It is clear to me that the sight of my face, revivified, in that symmetrical pool is a sign that I am to take the time to embrace body, soul, and all my experience; it is high time that I honor myself.

I never thought to celebrate myself, and particularly not my body—not even once—not after having sex for the first time, not after the births of our sons, not after nursing them through their young lives, not after the hundreds of times my arms were extended to console others. I—who talk and write about the importance of feminine energy with its warm vitality, its craving for ritual, its desire to embrace family, and its tremendous ability to carry the culture— have, because of my incessant doing, lost my feminine essence. I've been rushing forward in a straight line, pushing onward and upward to goals set most often by other people, against whom I've been measuring myself. When someone recently asked what ails me, I didn't have an answer, mostly because I refused to take the time to decipher the question. But just now I know what is missing in my life and what I crave to have back—an integration of my feminine and masculine aspects, that one doesn't overtake the other. I want a sense of balance that begins in my core.

I leave the mountaintop grateful for having traveled to a place whose culture reveres the stages and ages of human life as much as the passage of the seasons. The Celtic people saw a woman's experience as sacred. They did not denigrate a woman's aging but exalted it. I now have a glimmer of what is ahead of me and, what's more, just why I was driven to come here in the first place.

It is time to make my way back down the mountain, and I go almost skipping, able now to see my footing as well as the path. I am at the bottom in no time and walking jauntily toward town, slowing my step only when I notice that the Iona Book Shop, a tiny stucco building that is rarely open, has a light on and there is a vine of smoke coming out of its chimney. I peer through the window and see an artist at work. It must be the renowned wood-carver who specializes in Celtic crosses. I tap on the window, and he looks up from his workbench and motions me in.

"I won't disturb you, will I?" I ask and nod toward his work. "I've passed so many times and have been wanting to see your crosses." The rather large one he's working on is a commission for a church somewhere in England.

"Have a look around," he suggests, and I shuffle through chips of wood and newly honed curls, tiptoeing over piles of sawdust. On the walls, bookshelves, and ledges are crosses of every size and shape—some absolutely plain, others with intricate designs, all bearing the circle that appears to be the stabilizing element that adds strength to the four appendages.

"Why does the Celtic cross always have a circle?" I ask.

"It's the place where all the opposites come together," he says, never stopping for a minute from his work to look up. "There is another thought that it represents mother—the woman—who holds it all together." He smiles after this, and I wonder if he is being mildly sarcastic or if he believes the lore around the Goddess. Because he is so mild-mannered and with little inflection in his speech, I can't figure out if this is a man with a sense of humor or not.

"Don't usually see a hiker at this hour of the morning," he says. "Looks like you got yourself in the muck."

"That's easy to do around here." I laugh. "And going up to Dun-I, I had little choice. What they call a path is actually a mud slide."

"Indeed. Did you take pleasure in the vista?"

"How could I not?" I answer. "I saw the entire island and then the sunrise as well!"

"Where you were—Dun-I," he continues, looking up at me, his eyes great pools of blue water, "is really the island's intersection—like my crosses. You might have noticed that the island, because of its length and width, has the same proportions as a cross—we're three and a half miles long and one and a half miles wide—and it just about intersects at Dun-I."

I hadn't thought about the island's shape before, and his comment amazes me. I am also entranced by the design carved into many of his crosses—intertwined ropes, many of which look like two unbroken circles side by side. It is the symbol for infinity and, for me, reciprocity. His little studio also is smack in the middle of the island, at the edge of town, the gathering place for everyone, where real community thrives. Reciprocity, particularly on a small island, counts for everything. We can't live life alone.

"Very clever of you to begin your time here getting such perspective from Dun-I," he says. "But there's something in every corner."

"I've heard that going north brings healing, west offers patience, south, clarity, and I can't remember the quality one gets in the east."

"Grace," he tells me. "You'll find something wherever you walk."

I have always loved crosses, not for their religious connotations but because they are symbols of the crossroads—the four appendages representing four choices. Now I see that each appendage can also stand for direction, and if I take it further I am beginning to see that, in my own particular case, the four appendages could be my mother, two sons, and husband, with me "holding it together" in the center. I am drawn to a simple wooden cross designed to hang on a wall because it is uncomplicated, just like I want to become. But I'm also drawn to a more ornate freestanding one, etched with numerous Celtic images. Perhaps I will buy them both.

"Will you be here tomorrow?" I ask.

"Have been for the past twenty years," he answers. "Now that the season is upon us, I'll be open all day unless

I'm walking the dog," he says, pointing to the English shepherd asleep by the potbelly stove.

"It's been an honor meeting you," I say, taking my leave, my mind now reeling with the idea of hiking the entire island—walking the stages of the cross. I don't sense that this cross maker is a religious man, yet a gentle spirit emanates from him that must come from the repetitive work of chipping, peeling, honing, shaping, and eventually crafting one style of cross after another—like saying the rosary over and over again. I wonder how someone becomes a woodworker, or an artist of any kind for that matter. Here on Iona I'm told there is also one painter, a potter, and a jewelry designer. They obviously draw their inspiration not only from the physical beauty of this place but from its ancient culture. They do it, I suppose, to inspire—*inspirare* in the Latin means "to breathe life into what is true." As such they are silent preachers, letting their work speak instead of their words.

It seems each day offers another little epiphany on this island. You never know when your next angel, teacher, or mentor will appear. The glory of the experience is found in the element of surprise.

13

Yield

Late April

So to yield to life is to solve the unsolvable.

—*Lao Tzu*

*The idea of hiking the entire island deliberately and in each di-*rection never occurred to me before my woodworker friend affirmed the gifts available in each area of the "cross." But since I met him, the weather has been so horrific that for the past few days I have only been able to hike to the northern part of the island. Coincidentally that was precisely where I needed to go—to a place of healing. Although I had an enormous breakthrough on Dun-I in regards to the many facets of womanhood, I reflected, for the most part, on the miracle of my changing body, seeing only its glorious attributes—the yeoman's duty it had performed over the years. What I failed to take into account was the neglect it had endured, no thanks to me, and the fact that it had submitted its bill once again.

Currently it's my lower back that is crying out—the sacrum, it's called—short for "sacred," I muse. I find it interesting that the part of the spine that holds the pelvis together—the very place that holds new life—is giving me pain. I have basically shut it down, use it for very little now that my childbearing days are over, and aside from exercising it on my daily walks, I pretty much take it for granted. That and my shoulder blades, which are always in spasm because of "carrying the cross" as Louise Hay says, referring to women who readily carry everyone else's burdens. In any case, my backbone is in trouble—literally and figuratively. Which is why I hightailed it north in yesterday's unexpected short-lived blizzard. Still, several times I almost turned back. Bucking high winds did not seem the best prescription for healing. But I pushed on. Besides, one of the strange laws of contemplative life is that when you are in it you do not sit down and solve problems. Rather, you bear with them until somehow they solve themselves. During the past few days, I've sensed through one incidental experience after another that someone or something wants to find me, and that that something is my soul.

At first I was hesitant to even mention the word *soul* out loud—it sounded overwrought. Yet here on Iona, people toss the word around without a thought, perhaps because here, the soul is not the special provenance of organized religion. Indeed, soul is explained as nothing more than active imagination.

Iona has many secrets, and that is good. The walking paths are far from clear, and everything eventually meets up with the water. I'm reminded of Andrew Wyeth choosing Chadds Ford, Pennsylvania, to put down roots because he sensed everything that he would ever want to explore through painting could be found within a four-mile radius. Already, I sense that this is true here on Iona for me.

The fuel for my daily adventures comes from Katrina, the proprietress of the tiny grocery store not three doors away from my cottage. Every day I stop in, soon after she opens, to buy staples. I've missed female companionship, and she seems to enjoy bantering with her customers while stocking shelves, pricing goods, and tending to the cash register. Besides, she knows everything about this island and its people.

Today when I stop by to pick up some items for my picnic, she asks, "And where might you be going today?" clearly pleased that I have taken to her island with such gusto.

"Not sure," I answer, looking over the fruit. As is true on any island, it has been in the store a day too long, so I pass on the plums and move on to the cheese. "I went north yesterday—much more glorious than any beach we have on Cape Cod. I am quickly losing my skepticism. It was a tough walk—against the wind all the way—but well worth it. I went out with a tight lower back, and look at me now," I say, proudly upright with a new kick in my step.

"Aye, walking north will heal whatever ails you," she answers, not at all surprised.

"I brought back handfuls of beach glass, too. You can just reach in and pull it out in any imaginable color."

"If that strikes your fancy, then you'll be needing to go west," she says, "to the beach at the back of the bay—there are thousands of stones like this," she says, pulling out from under the counter a magnificent beige stone with a brilliant white circle on each end. "Here, touch it," she continues, placing it in the palm of my hand. Within seconds it becomes warm.

"My island is made up of the most ancient rock on earth," she continues with pride. "It's a geological fact. We have not only special rocks but also green marble," she says, pointing to a case full of jewelry made by a local artisan—polished green gems in all sizes and shapes. "Beautiful, aye? These rocks and marble hold the voices of our ancestors and saints. They live in the ground, y'know, and in the moors, even in the sea, especially to the west. Their voices help you find the gifts."

Stones that talk? She must be kidding. Still I believe her in some odd way. Katrina clearly delights in stirring up the imagination.

"I bet you found a good spot to cozy up out there in the north," she continues, as I begin loading my basket with rolls, cheese, smoked salmon, pâté, water, and a half bottle of white wine.

"As a matter of fact I did," I admit, "a wonderful natural seat hollowed out of a boulder, nicely covered with moss. I tucked in and stared at the land as it stretched out to the very edge of the sea until I fell fast asleep."

"The medicine seeps right up from under you." She sounds almost like a seer, but when I put my stash on the counter, she readily turns back into a clerk. Old Greek legends depict fleeting encounters with messengers on the road, insisting that the sacred is often hidden in the commonplace. Could that mean even a grocery store? Anxious now to get going, I gather my supplies and head out. "See you tomorrow then," I say.

A woman who had been lingering in the shop follows right behind me. "I couldn't help overhearing your conversation," she says with a thick Irish brogue. "I'm heading west myself. Would you like some company? I could get you to just the right spot."

I hesitate. Although I've been getting a lot out of staying with my own thoughts, serendipitous encounters seem to be opening many doors. Besides there is something sparkling and elflike about this woman, and I find myself saying yes. "I'd be delighted," I say, extending my hand around the bag of groceries. "My name is Joan—Joan Anderson."

"I'm Dolores Whelan," she says. "It's most refreshing to feel your interest in this place. It's one of my favorites. So then, shall we meet up in, say, a half hour?"

"Perfect. My cottage is that one, over there," I say, pointing it out. "Until then," I say, and off she goes.

HALF PAST THE HOUR, Dolores appears on my doorstep, and we move quickly up the hill and out of town, onto a dirt path that takes us over a rather steep incline. I am huffing and puffing in minutes, while Dolores is busy chattering. "Life is rugged here," she says, as we pass through a cluttered barnyard full of makeshift farm equipment, piled up fish traps, a few bales of last year's hay crop, and some small, three-wheeled vehicles designed for the craggy terrain. "But the place is fierce with reality, wouldn't you say? Most of the world is illusion, but Iona is real. That's why I keep coming back."

"How often have you been here?" I ask.

"Six or seven times. I was a scientist in my past life, but I got so filled up with logic and mind games that I had no choice but to find something more to believe in. Being Irish, the Celtic way of thinking caught my fancy. They are, after all, my ancestors. And you?"

"My father insisted that everyone should visit this place. So when I received an invitation from an absolute stranger, I knew I had to accept."

She gives me a pat on the back and offers a knowing smile as we step onto the one-lane road that leads to the Bay at the Back of the Ocean. "What do you do?" she shouts over the strong winds.

"I'm a writer—I wrote a couple of books for women about finding their real selves as opposed to the people everyone wants them to be. But somehow in the process of promoting my idea I got off track and was in need of rescue."

"You've come to the right place," she assures me. "You know the Celtic people had spread themselves all over Europe until the Romans chased them away. They moved farther and farther north and then to the west looking for inaccessible places to live, places where they might be able to preserve what they knew. Go someplace remote and no one will bother you. That's what we've done, right?" she jokes, almost skipping along now like a happy child. "I am a writer, too," she says nonchalantly. "My first book was called *The Breaking Point*."

"Sounds like I should get a copy."

She's a sturdy woman with a pixie face and a jovial manner, eager not to take herself, or anyone, too seriously, both humble and open.

"You've chosen the perfect time to come," she continues,

as we pass a field of daffodils, somehow revived after the last few days of frost. "Spring is the time of the maiden—youth, the planting of new seeds, and the beginning of everything."

"Sounds good to me," I answer. "I'm celebrating the end of a decade—and, I hope, the beginning of something new." She is kind enough not to ask what that might be, and we both sink into silence for a while until I need to stop, pull my hood around my head, and zip up my jacket as far as it will go. Minutes later we are crossing a meadow that also serves as a pasture and a golf course. Beyond it, I see the most magnificent cove and a glimpse of the Atlantic, which today looks like the Caribbean—a deep aqua hue with frilly white surf rushing toward shore and onto rocks piled so high they must have washed ashore centuries ago.

"Here's where we part. Try to scramble up that moor. You'll warm up in no time," she says, pointing to what appears to be a mountain, not a hill. "There's the most beautiful view. You can see clear across to Ireland! Keep moving or tuck in behind a boulder. We could meet up at lunchtime, if you like. There's a brilliant cave along the farthest end of the shore. Until then?"

With that she's off, moving like a mountain goat, climbing the moor she insisted I climb. Within minutes I see her standing on top, perilously close to the edge, arms extended, looking like an eagle about to soar. I'm reminded of a line from Hebrews that goes something like this:"Don't forget to be kind to strangers, for some who have done this have entertained angels without realizing it."

I ramble on, toward the shore, passing myriad stone sculptures as I go—stones in the shape of fish, a heart, intertwined circles—and numerous cairns. Just as Katrina had told me, the entire shoreline is piled six or seven feet high with rocks. I am moved by the sound of water as it rushes over and under these rounded stones and then draws back in a thunderous roar.

I never really cared about stones before and much preferred collecting shells whenever I was at the beach. But knowing that this island is made up of some of the most ancient rock in the world, I find myself looking at them in a new way. In no time, the stones become like gems, and I want them all. Soon I am on all fours, studying their sizes and shapes.

Where did they come from? And how long did it take for them to become so smooth, so intricately shaped, so perfect in their imperfections? When I look closely, I can see their distinguishing features—their subtle shades of brown, white, gray, black, and I recognize that each seems to carry its own message. I pick up an egg-shaped stone made from the famed green marble and tuck it into my backpack. It will be the symbol of my hatching. There are several heart-shaped ones, and I grab as many as I dare carry—one for my husband, two more, representing my sons and their families, and a pink-speckled one that speaks of my reawakened self. There is a gray rock in the shape of a perfect circle with a white stripe around its side. That shall sit on my desk back home and remind me that I have come full circle. The black rock with a perfect line coiling to its center will remind me that I am forever to spiral into myself and then spiral out with what I've learned. With my pack full to bursting I leave it behind while I stroll over to a nearby moor.

It is complicated getting from the rocks to the moor. I must scale two large boulders, dip down into a valley, and then climb over a barbed-wire fence. I am sweating and a little breathless, but after rounding the bend, I see my father—not actually him, but the ghost of him for certain—walking jauntily up one glen and down another, appearing and disappearing, his tattered, moth-eaten kilt swinging in the breeze, singing his favorite Harry Lauder tune: "Roamin' in the gloamin'. . . . Oh, it's lovely roamin' in the gloamin' ."

It is indeed, Daddy, I say to myself. *You made me get here, didn't you? Somehow you knew that I was stuck and such a place would be my tonic.* I want more than anything to hear his booming voice again—to see him in all his glory. He was a simple yet complicated man, whose wisdom, I am beginning to understand, came from his heritage. "You can't take it with you," he was always saying. "Don't hesitate. Take the moment when it comes." I chase after him and catch him taking a swig of Scotch from his flask—"A wee drop to ward off the chill," he'd say. "Stand sure, my girlie," he'd shout, whenever he felt I was afraid or didn't want to risk something. The ghost looks up, and I swear he catches my eye. I can almost hear him saying, "You'll find all you need to know to carry you through on this little island."

Then, just as suddenly as he appeared, he is gone. Once

again, I'm reminded that in the Celtic tradition a person is born through three forces: the coming together of mother and father; an ancestral spirit's wish to be reborn; and the involvement of the God or Goddess. Just now, I feel that I have met my father's spirit wishing somehow to be reborn through me.

It is starting to sprinkle. I walk back to my pack and don my slicker, as a squall pours out of the dark hills. I run in the direction of the purported cave, down the sodden beach, looking furiously for any sort of indentation in the nearby cliff that would signal a cave. With rain drenching my cheeks I am certain I must be headed in the wrong direction. But a few steps later, just where the shoreline bends, there it is—a large opening and a floor made of pure white sand.

Although most caves feel dark, gloomy, and claustrophobic to me, this one is shallow, bright, and inviting. I step into the pear-shaped crevice that has been carved by time and the sea, and feel safe. It is as if an artist painted its various rock formations in shades of red, maroon, and purple, with accents of blue, green, and shiny black. Although the ceiling is high and I am able to maneuver about, this haven beckons me to sit, relax, and take shelter in its confines. I am of course reminded of a womb, as storytellers have long since seen the cave as its metaphor. But what astonishes me as I gaze at these walls is the beauty of the interior. I sit down cross-legged, happy to wait out the tide.

"Hello there," Dolores says, not ten minutes later, shocking me with her intrusion as she ducks in out of the rain and pats the side of the wall. "Quite a spot I found for us, aye, quintessentially feminine, right? God is good, that's for sure, but he had a great mother," she says, chortling at her strange humor. "All substance and form comes out of a dark place, y'know. Good thing to reflect upon in spring, when we get ready to plant our seeds."

I smile at her uncomplicated wisdom as she takes out a thermos of tea and has a swig, then unwraps a huge sandwich of hummus, tomato, cheese, and sprouts. I lean back on the wall and surrender to the interlude, rendered speechless. This is everything I had hoped for and more but, at the same time, too much—the earth energy, meeting up with my father, and now actually succumbing to my feminine self in this cave. To live wholly or holy is not to reach for some otherness but to penetrate deeply into each moment, hour, or season. Something invisible is happening, and it has come this time from simply following my instinct and being patient. I sit up, realizing that patience is what this beach to the west is meant to teach. It is funny how conversion experiences begin with a gentle rub—they are intuitive, like me saying yes to Dolores today. If you are lucky, the journey is full of surprises. In this brief time on Iona, I've come to feel sad for the person who needs a well-marked trail.

"Looks like we will be here for a bit." Dolores breaks the silence. "Have to wait out the tide or else get awfully wet."

Another exercise in patience, I think. "I could stand a little nap," I say, and without waiting for her opinion, I curl up with my backpack as a pillow and drift off.

Hours later I awaken to the bright sun and a tide pulled

out to sea, leaving behind it a sweeping beach of white sand just outside the cave door. Dolores is nowhere to be found. She did, however, leave a note on my pack:

> There will never be peace without tapping into the
> spiritual realm.
> May the delight of this day continue.
>
> Dolores

Knowing the elf that she is, I sense our paths will cross again.

WITH THE AFTERNOON only partially used up, I decide to push on, not back to town and the grace I might find by walking east, but south, for the clarity that surely awaits me at Columba's Bay. I have been dying to go there ever since I learned it is the very spot where St. Columba—the sixth-century Irish priest who brought Christianity to Iona—landed. He was liberal enough to blend the teachings of Catholicism with the philosophies of the Druids and the Celts. Since so much of the spirit of Iona originates in this tiny monk's goodness and unconventionality, and knowing that clarity awaits the pilgrim who walks south, I eagerly take my crumpled map out of my pocket to assess the distance from here to there.

It looks as if Columba's Bay can't be more than a mile or two. I've never had a good sense of direction, but for some reason I have had an easier time finding my way here on Iona. The place is so small and therefore somewhat manageable, but I suspect it has something to do with how focused and on track I've become—no longer just guessing as to which way my life is to go but walking in a set direction full of clear intentions.

Just out of the cave, I spot a well-trodden path that leads up over the first moor. The terrain quickly becomes complicated, and the pack full of rocks on my back is cumbersome. But I push on, over inviting little wooden footbridges, onto a path created by flattened rocks, past a lake full of swans, dormant heather, and the crackly silver grasses that are trying to become green.

"Give me a wildness whose glance no civilization can endure," said Thoreau, and I couldn't agree with him more. The environment's ruggedness and purity feel abundantly soothing; that is, until I have to navigate muddy spots like the one I suddenly see up ahead.

I head for a dried-out-looking bog, but when I step down, I realize it, too, is wet earth. I sink into muck so thick that I almost lose my boot to it. Instead of cursing, I find myself laughing at my foolishness. By now, I should know how easy it is to get stuck in the muck, especially when you are trying to follow a shortcut. Nothing worthwhile can be hurried— not the seasons, not birth or death, the coming of day, the moving into night; not a composition, a thought, a work of art, or the form of a story. Patience is what makes each experience meaningful. Finding the time to be patient is what makes a life well lived. I pull myself out of my mess yet again, take some paper towels from my pack to wipe the slop off my legs, and move on toward a promontory not far off.

Once there, I lean on my stick and gaze at the sweeping view of Columba's Bay—lush green grass spreading out like a carpet to the white sand. Beyond the sand, emerald green water heaves gently up and around the numerous little islands that dot its surface. In the distance I hear the unmistakable barking of seals and follow the sound out onto an island where they are lolling about on the rocks. The water between the shore and them is shallow, but I approach slowly so as not to slip on the slimy boulders and scare the animals off. The seals stay put, turning their heads in unison and greeting me with their soulful eyes when I am a mere two boulders away. It is one thing to be in the presence, even for a second, of a wild creature and yet another to be welcomed into their pod. I truly feel that I am in a place out of time. I sit with the seals, silently watching their fat, sleek bodies jostle against one another and the water rush in and out of the crevices between the rocks. After a time, a mist shrouds everything and I feel chilled. The sun has fallen behind a bank of clouds; it is time to move on. As I reach higher ground, I turn to take one last look at the entire cove and am surprised to see a detail I hadn't noticed before. Among the many small cairns and larger monuments made of rock, I see a rather large and curious-looking circle of stones. I walk over to the spot and am stunned to find a labyrinth, half buried under grass.

Such ancient circles, designed as meditative tools some four thousand years ago, are often found in churches, gardens, sacred sites, vortexes, but I've yet to stumble upon a labyrinth in the wild.

Still, nothing I happen upon on Iona should surprise me anymore, and what's more I have learned to accept any such gift that this island offers. So, although it has once again started to rain—not just a Scottish mist but actual drops—I know I must walk into this sacred spiral that is surely a metaphor for the path I am on. If indeed I am intent upon changing my life, not just resuming it, then walking the labyrinth could offer the very impetus I need.

In no time I find the entrance and then notice that there is a cairn of stones in the center. It seems that those who walk the labyrinth are meant to leave something of themselves in the center. I spot a pure white round stone, clutch it in my palm, take a few deep breaths, and step onto the grassy path as I enter into this silent sanctuary. Putting one foot in front of the other, I feel like the child I once was playing bride or fairy princess in the backyard, oblivious to anyone or anything save a cacophony of soothing sounds— the tide rushing in, surf breaking fast, honking gulls, and of course my barking seals—all of which force me to surrender further to the process.

It takes all manner of concentration not to lose my footing on such a narrow path, but this simple journey miraculously stifles all mindless chatter and I once again become totally present. Walking the path renders me deliberate and patient. Slowing down the body in such a way seems to help in the stirring up of the soul.

This is no maze set with tricks and dead ends. All roads lead to the center. There is just one way in and one way out, unless of course I would cheat by stepping over or across one path to another. But that would defeat the purpose of this walk. There is no shortchanging the route to clarity—it does require balance, patience, and the willingness to take the time to risk.

For a split second I feel self-conscious and look around at who might be observing me as I partake in this mini-ritual. But then I laugh at myself—remembering that I am, after all, on a vacant beach somewhere in the Hebrides, where no one is watching save the seals, a few goats, and multiple sheep. And so, I further relax into the experience, grateful for all the steps I have taken on this Iona journey. Once in the center, I am blessed with an inner peace for which I have no words. I am once again reminded of the Anderson motto: "Stand Sure," and do just that, pulling my shoulders back, breathing in the mystical air, feeling the earth's energy seep upward from the ground until it fills my entire being. I gaze at the circle in which I am enclosed and know that there is no beginning or end to any circle—the circle is symbolic of life and as such consists of one endless continuum.

Placing my stone on top of the pile, I watch for it to tumble, but instead it stays put in its precarious spot—not unlike me right now, reaching for new heights, counting on my foundation to support new ventures. The restlessness I have been feeling—the lack of grounding as I pushed outward in search of harmony—has been soothed at last by this sacred moment. This entire journey has drawn me into a labyrinth of sacred confusion where, in becoming innocent once again, I have been able to discover so many aspects of myself, once buried and lost. At the beginning of this pilgrimage, I had sought healing—to be restored to health, soundness, and spiritual wholeness—and that has been gifted to me here because I've been open, receptive, and patient. I no longer require a wished-for future to cancel out the present. All that I have here and now is enough.

Nothing happens overnight. Developing a relationship with the unknown takes time. In doing so the seeker is granted the greatest gift of all—clarity. I have come full circle yet again. I must always be willing to journey forward—spiral into the center and then back out again. Then and only then will I be whole, in touch with all that I am.

14

Unfinished Journey

Late April

It is time I came back to my real life
After this voyage to an island with no name,
Where I lay down at sunrise drunk with light.

—*May Sarton*

The ever-faithful ferry is making one of its last crossings of the day. Up until now, I've felt smug watching people come and go, knowing that I had settled in and become part of this little island. But alas, all good things must come to an end, and tomorrow I leave. That is why I'm at my writer's table, sipping a glass of port and trying to capture the many thoughts I have about what this experience has meant.

Somewhere down the street a fiddler is playing a very merry Celtic tune that sounds like something from *Riverdance*. I stop writing and gaze out the window, drinking in the fading day as the sun drops somewhere into the sea. "On Iona," wrote Kenneth Steven, "what matters is conquering the wind, coming home dry shod, getting the fire lit. I am not sure whether there is no time here or more time, whether the light is stronger or just easier to see." Well, Mr. Steven, I'm not sure, either. I write:

> I feel as though I've awakened from a dream. A mere three weeks ago, I crossed over to a fabled kingdom, found myself in a trance, wandered about like a man on the moon, uninterrupted except for a few incidental meetings which led me on to the next destination, a sort of connect-the-dot existence.

Something invisible happened here. Isn't that the way with adult growth—a shift here, a change there? One day, for whatever reason, you wake up and no longer are who you were the day before. Because Iona is so removed from the ordinary, it provides a fertile field for pure thought, original ideas, and one's own salvation to blossom. Joseph Campbell professed: "You must have a place to which you can go in your heart, your mind, or your house, almost every day, where you do not owe anyone and where no one owes you—a place that simply allows for the blossoming of something new and promising." Iona has been that place apart for me.

It seemed that I had come here to pursue wholeness—to find a way out of the fragmentation and entanglement that had come to define my life. Here, I found simplicity. I faced elemental challenges such as rain, sleet, and fierce wind, but I found respite from all the distractions and self-imposed pressures of my life at home. More than anything else, it is the people—the islanders I have watched creating their lives, not just letting them happen—who have helped me see what really matters.

I lay down my pen and gaze out the window at the little village, bustling at day's end—women scurrying to market, farmers herding their sheep from one field to another, several fishing boats trying to anchor in the rough channel. Everyone on an island is a cog in the wheel, working for the good of the whole, not just the success of the individual. What's more, most of the people know just what is expected of them each day—how much they need to accomplish and when they can turn to other endeavors, vocations, or hobbies. I leave the island with the hope that those demands that continue to rear their ugly heads—things such as guilt, speed, perfectionism—will dissipate as I remember Iona and the life I experienced here.

Just now I need to pack my bags. I toss mostly soiled clothing into my backpack, wrapping several purchases—a mug from the Iona Pottery Shop, a piece of stained glass from the abbey, and of course, my coveted hand-carved cross—in sweaters and jerseys. The last is to remind me to walk in each direction, being patient rather than impatient, searching for clarity when I find myself confused, and knowing, in the end, that although I can't arrange for grace to happen, it will be mine if I remain true to myself.

A quick check through the staples in Mrs. MacDonald's kitchen reminds me I have several things to replace, so I toss on my sweater and head off for the grocery store before it closes.

"You'll be leaving us in the morrow?" Katrina asks without emotion.

"Yes," I answer directly, though her question makes me swallow. "And I'm not happy about it in the least."

"Will ye not be back again?" she pushes.

"Oh, I'll be back," I say, now looking at the woolen caps and T-shirts that say "Iona," and tossing several of each, along with a dozen postcards, into my basket.

"And did you find what you were looking for?" she asks.

"Indeed, and more as well." I take a small heart-shaped stone out of my pocket and lay it on the counter. "Found this at the back of the bay and thought of you," I say. "Thanks for pointing the way."

Katrina blushes and dips her chin. As several other people have entered the store, she retreats behind the counter.

"That'll do," I say, laying my purchases on the counter. "Oh, and would you mind adding a bottle of single malt as well as a bottle of your best port?"

"Feeling flush, are ye?"

"Just grateful," I answer.

"Twenty-two pounds thirty," she says succinctly. I know she is reluctant to show any emotion, so I refrain from giving her a hug. But the handshake seems too cold and too little.

"You'll be coming to the ceilidh [pronounced kay-lee] tonight?" she asks.

"The what?"

"It's a gathering of all the islanders at the village hall. We have one at the beginning and end of every season," she explains. "There'll be singing and dancing. The Argyll is catering the food. It should be brilliant."

"But I'm not an islander," I say with some confusion.

"You might as well be. After living here for three weeks, no one refers to you as the American anymore now, do they? It would be a nice chance for you to say good-bye."

Certainly I don't have anything else planned for tonight,

and she is being uncharacteristically insistent. "All right then," I answer. "What time?"

"Seven o'clock," she says with a smile.

SEVERAL HOURS LATER, after digging my one skirt out of my backpack, I pull a newly purchased tartan shawl over my shoulders, fluff up my hair, and head toward the sound of the music and the smell of a barbecue. Daniel and his staff are just setting out the food—a roasted pig, several salads, lots of potatoes, and of course, shortbread for dessert. Inside someone's made an attempt to brighten the rather grimly painted walls and dark woodwork by stringing multi-colored Christmas lights back and forth across the ceiling. The place is packed—all the seats are taken along the walls, and the few tables and chairs filled with hungry fishermen and farmers, clearly eager to start gobbling the well-cooked food. I feel the need to tell someone that I was actually invited, as I survey the room to see who I know. There isn't one familiar face, so I head for the door just as Dolores appears. "God, it's good to see you," I say. "I'd hoped we'd have another hike, but my time is up."

"So you're leaving, are you? Pity."

"First thing in the morning," I tell her. "Katrina suggested that this might be a good way to exit. I've never been to a ceilidh before," I say.

"You're in for a treat then," she says, eyeing my feet. "I'm glad to see you have flat shoes on. Things can get pretty wild."

"I'm not going to have to dance, am I?"

"If you're in the room, someone'll find you. More men than women on this island. Dare say, you'll have a partner in no time."

I feel my stomach turn. I came to observe, not participate.

"Let's get a drink," she suggests, ordering a pint for herself. "What will you have?"

"A dram," I say boldly. "I hear it's called Scottish communion."

"Good choice—it'll loosen you up for what's to come," she says as we head for the bar and she plunks down a couple of pounds. "My treat!"

It's one of those damp, heavy nights. We move toward one of the open doors to catch a breeze. But even here at the edge of the crowd, it is getting harder to talk. An assortment of musicians has gathered on the stage and begun tuning up fiddles, flutes, whistles, and an accordion. "Oh my God," Dolores all but gasps as she watches a woman take the stage. "Fiona's here. She's the most amazing bard—one of the best."

A deep hush descends upon the room as everyone notices the presence of this rather tall eccentric woman with red hair, who seems to be about my age. "She sings fairy music," Dolores whispers. "You'll absolutely fall in love with her."

Sitting down on a chair that has been placed there for her, Fiona takes up her ancient harp and then waits for the hall to become still, clearly a woman in command of her audience. Warming up, she picks at the harp until a tune begins to take shape, as if she were improvising, and yet the music is already melodic with the power to lull me into a trance. In time she begins to sing, ever so softly at first, her deep contralto voice soothing and rich. I close my eyes and listen to the lyrics—songs of longing, songs of joy, but mostly songs of Scotland, her beloved home. I don't ever want her to stop. In closing, she sings of a wise woman.

Woman of the wisdom tree
Goddess of humanity
Singing of the unity we long for.
Made of eternity
Naked in her mystery
Singing of the unity we long for.
Fierce and gentle
Wild and brave
Simple in her majesty
Daring in the unity we long for.

There is gentle applause, as if the audience has emerged from the same trance as I have.

"Didn't I tell you she was brilliant?" Dolores interrupts. "To me she embodies the hag."

"A hag!" I look at Dolores aghast. "How could you call her that?"

"Because it's a compliment," Dolores says. "In Gaelic, we call a woman of her age and stature the *cailleach*—the older woman who is powerful and highly sure of herself. She has no need of adoration from others. She knows who she is—kind of like you, Joan, the hag!" she says, shouting now above the band, which has just started playing, as the floor fills with dancing couples.

"Hags are of great interest to our men, you know," Dolores chides. "I've heard them whispering about you since I've been here. They're fascinated by how you've taken to the island."

"I think I'll have another dram," I say and head back to the bar, a mistake I realize, as I am stopped on my way by an older gentleman and asked to join one of the squares. The music is frenetic and the dancing more lively than I had anticipated, and we move with dizzying speed. I make a weak attempt to hop on my left foot, step on the right, then hop twice and step three times. But I soon abandon the effort and just move. We dance in a line, each holding on to the person in front of us. When you reach the end, you get flung from one dancer to another, as in a game of the Whip. I'm caught by one man just seconds before landing on the floor. Red-faced and dripping with perspiration, I am grateful when this endurance test comes to an end, and I duck outside for some fresh air.

Through the window I peer back into the room and spot several of those who unknowingly pointed the way—tossed a pebble into the pool of my wisdom. There is the woodworker, sitting alone in the corner sipping a pint; Katrina, clutching the shawl wrapped around her shoulders eyeing the couples but somehow not interested in being one; Daniel, embracing everyone, always the island's consummate concierge; and of course, Dolores, innocent, unaffected, eager as a child to be a part of almost anything. Coming here, I felt certain that I could, to paraphrase the theologian Frederick Buechner, "survive on my own, grow on my own, even prevail on my own," but in the end, as he said, "you cannot become human on your own." For that, I will always need the serendipitous gifts that come from strangers along the road.

It is starting to drizzle and I am ready for bed. I make my way up the dark street toward the cottage, knowing that I am stumbling in the right direction now.

THE ALARM GOES OFF AT SIX, and I am up and out of the cottage in fewer than twenty minutes. Already several others are hurrying toward the dock, suitcases being wheeled behind them, but I hang back a bit and cherish my solitude. Saying good-bye to the island is a challenge. "We must meet the unknown future by bringing to bear everything that has been shaped by us in the past," said the Irish writer John O'Donohue. For me, the immediate future will, no doubt, be shaped by the spirit of Iona. I arrived here with hard-won external strengths, but I leave with invaluable internal ones—humility, patience, grace, clarity, and integrity, to name a few. Each day here, I lived fully, without rushing to anticipate tomorrow and without working to make tomorrow better than today. As a result, I am excited about, but also patient with, all that is still unsolved in my heart.

I notice a piper heading toward the pier and wonder which of the travelers is being given the royal send-off. Not a minute later Katrina pops out of her store, followed by Dolores, both running now, as the ferry is halfway across the channel. Dolores hugs me and presses into the palm of my hand a brass bookmark in the shape of a figure eight. "Now is the time and we are the ones we have been waiting for," she whispers. Then Katrina approaches and hands me her gift, a piece of Iona marble, hanging from a leather chain. "Will ye nay come back again," she says quickly and, without waiting for an answer, turns and runs off.

As the plank is lowered onto the pier and eager passengers scurry aboard, the piper begins to play "Scotland the Brave." I march onward, remembering the ballad sung by Fiona the night before, and believing that I, too, am a woman of the wisdom tree, fierce and gentle, wise and brave. After tucking my pack into a hold, I rush to the upper deck to watch, for the last time, my Iona fade from view.

As the engines grind and we back away from shore, I realize that all such journeys end with arrival somewhere. One hopes there is some manner of resolution and closure for the pilgrim—a new slate upon which to design her next phase. Blessed with a quiet peace as I stand at the rail, I feel ready to spiral outward yet grateful that the journey home will take as long as the journey inward, granting me time for further thought.

As the sound of the bagpipes fades into the mist, I stand sure, as the Anderson motto proclaims, and tip my hat to a father who knew best the value of drawing on heritage and history. I can feel the ancestral spirits waiting to be reborn, and I wish to do them proud. To that end I take out of my pocket a little piece of paper on which I've written a few new instructions that will help me stay the new course—those new ideals that came from my various conversion experiences:

> Embrace change—knowing that life is always
>   being reconfigured.
> Befriend the person you are striving to become.
> Welcome new paths. Enjoy the detours.
> Strive to go deeper rather than just forward.
> Know that most unnecessary demands come from
>   the unfinished parts of self.
> Beware of speed. It is often one's undoing.
> Wholehearted is the way. Halfhearted will kill you.
> Harness your evolvement.
> Let go of what is outlived to make room for
>   the unlived.

As my special island becomes a mere blur on the horizon, I become aware that this particular "second journey" is over, but a new decade looms in front of me. I welcome the course ahead. For if I have learned nothing else, it is that the journey will always be unfinished.

Understanding the Journey

To translate the work of a second journey in your own life I have included descriptions of the various journeys as I have experienced them. Being aware of such "roads" allows the pilgrim intent upon redefining her life to have a more rewarding experience. Be it fortune or misfortune that sets you on your course, the road is never straight. But it is through trial and error as well as conflicts and resolutions that the path is made all the more significant. And so I wish you Bon Voyage!

Second Journeys

Second journeys most often commence in midlife, when the power of youth is gone and the dreams of earlier years turn out to be shallow and pointless. For a woman, this is frequently a time to find her more personal worth, beyond that of mother and wife. By merely acknowledging her ache, recognizing that it comes from knowing there is something bigger, better, and more life-giving to strive for, a woman begins a process of individuation once again. It is as if Sleeping Beauty has been awakened, not by a kiss from a prince but because she has decided to be a participant in her own life rather than remain a victim of experience. Second journeys demand that one move away from the familiar—isolate, relocate, and return new to an old place. In the process, a woman learns to walk alongside herself, once again. It is a decision one makes to end stagnation and become more generative—to eventually feel as though one is reborn, that one's life is finally freshly beginning again. Strange as it seems, an end always creates a beginning.

Accidental Journeys

Accidental journeys are unexpected interludes that can heighten a woman's journey but also pull her off course. Alice in Wonderland experiences such a journey when, out of boredom, she chases a rabbit down its hole and is confronted with myriad challenges, surprises, traps, and bad advice. On an accidental journey, a woman might find herself traveling unfamiliar roads that were never meant to be on her itinerary. Such journeys take many forms, but they always begin in innocence and with an element of surprise. Whatever the specifics, we usually find that we have taken a wrong turn, overstayed our welcome, and we eventually decide to get back on track.

Counterfeit Journeys

Counterfeit journeys are alluring. They happen when we are willing to compromise our values out of desperation, wanting, lust, or pride. Usually we are looking for some shortcut to happiness, a quick fix to free us from empty and barren times, a chance to make big money or buy happiness or even love. We may have been able to glimpse what is true and right but lacked the courage or principle to back off. At the end of such a journey we are left feeling like a fraud, shamed that we've "sold our souls for a mess of pottage." Worse still, we know that we have betrayed our very selves. Undoing the remnants of a counterfeit journey can take a very long time.

Spiritual Journeys

Spiritual journeys begin with a "call," an irresistible pull to find our higher self. We find that we are experiencing a sacred restlessness, which stems from the fact that we long for truth, intimacy, and being at one with self and soul. Such journeys can commence with a pilgrimage—an adventure into the wilderness, a retreat with soulful advisers. The intent of such journeys is to wrest meaning from meaninglessness, find a revised sense of purpose, and create a new consciousness about life that depends more on fulfilling our inner needs than satisfying our outer desires.

The Second Journey Itinerary

*Some thirty years ago I found a small book on my mother's book-*shelf that intrigued me. It was written by a Roman Catholic priest and was called *The Second Journey: Spiritual Awareness and the Mid-Life Crisis.* I was neither in crisis nor middle-aged, but something resonated with me. What was I going to do once the children were launched and the rest of my life was laid out before me? I devoured the book the day I found it and have read it numerous times since. In it, Gerald O'Collins attempts to address life's meaning beyond the time when we are involved in family and careers. He explains that the first journey concerns performing the expected roles and the third journey is about old age and life's ending. But there is that big stretch of time in the middle! What are we meant to do with our wisdom and vitality during our middle years?

He was able to lay out a rough itinerary of how and why one embarks on such a journey and then he offered the pattern that follows.

1. Change is thrust upon you.

2. You experience a crisis of feelings.

3. Having been stopped, you must take an
    outer journey.

4. Being alone for a time creates change:
    a reversal of values and goals.

5. Suddenly you feel alone. You've changed
    but the world hasn't.

6.   A longer period of isolation and
    exploration follows.

7. You become at home with your new self and
    gain wisdom and power.

Adapted from Gerald O'Collins,
*The Second Journey: Spiritual
Awareness and the Mid-Life Crisis*,
Paulist Press, 1978 (out of print).

THE SECOND JOURNEY ITINERARY

**CHANGE THRUST
UPON YOU**

Transitions

Unresolved conflicts

Personal failure

Bad diagnosis

CRISIS OF FEELINGS

No way around

Desperation

*Overcome with
haunting feelings*

OUTER JOURNEY

Time out

Restlessness

A stopping

To be finished

**A REVERSAL OF
MEANINGS,
GOALS, VALUES**

*A reversal of all
cherished ideals*

*A new sense of what
is real and true*

End of illusion

LONELINESS

No one shares my feelings

I am traveling alone

The route is uncharted

*Friends and family
don't understand and even
abandon me*

WISDOM AND POWER

Regain equilibrium

*Find a way toward
fresh purpose*

New dreams

Happily become a solitaire

Feel original